The Korean Economy

The Korean Economy: From Growth to Maturity takes an in-depth, amalgamated look at the evolution of Korea's globalization drive from the early 2000s (Kim Dae-jung regime, 1998–2003) to the present period (Park Geun-hye, 2013–2017). The book discusses the role of foreign companies on the sustainability of Korea's economic growth, the relationship between the *chaebol* and the MNCs, the evolution of Korea's nation brand, and the role of the state in Korea's new economic trajectory (globalization) since the 2000s.

With data collected from fieldwork, the book provides both empirical and qualitative insights (economic, socio-cultural and political economic analysis) into the Korean political economy and would be a very useful reference to other emerging economies experiencing similar globalization paths.

You-il Lee is Associate Professor of International Business and Director of the King Sejong Institute Adelaide at the University of South Australia. You-il is a political economist and has published research on socio-economic and political changes caused by globalization and regionalism in Asia. He has published widely in leading journals in the areas of Asian Studies, Asian business management and Asian political economy. His latest book (co-authored) is *The Political Economy of New Regionalism in Northeast Asia: Dynamics and Contradictions* (2018). You-il is currently working on a further monograph, entitled *The Impact of Foreign Multinational Corporations in Korea*. He has taught and coordinated courses on Asian political economy, international business/management, and cross-cultural management, and currently teaches post-graduate courses as part of the UniSA Business School's 5-star MBA and International MBA programs.

Richard Lee is Associate Professor of Marketing and Associate Director for the Australian Centre for Asian Business at the University of South Australia. Prior to joining UniSA in 2007, Richard spent 15 years managing sales and marketing functions with Asian IT/telecommunication companies. His research expertise is in international and ethnic marketing, with particular focus on Asian markets. His publications have appeared in the *European Journal of Marketing*, *Journal of International Marketing* and *International Marketing Review*. Richard has also won several industry grants that focus on how Australian SMEs can capitalize on free-trade agreements and on enhancing the export competitiveness of Australian food and wine companies. His teaching experience includes consumer behaviour, marketing planning, customer relationship management and market research.

Routledge Studies in the Modern World Economy

For more information about this series, please visit www.routledge.com/Routledge-Studies-in-the-Modern-World-Economy/book-series/SE0432

The Korean Economy
From Growth to Maturity

You-il Lee and Richard Lee

LONDON AND NEW YORK

First published 2019
by Routledge
2 Park Square, Milton Park, Abingdon, Oxon OX14 4RN

and by Routledge
52 Vanderbilt Avenue, New York, NY 10017

Routledge is an imprint of the Taylor & Francis Group, an informa business

First issued in paperback 2021

British Library Cataloguing-in-Publication Data
A catalogue record for this book is available from the British Library

Library of Congress Cataloging-in-Publication Data
Names: Lee, You-Il, author. | Lee, Richard, 1961- author.
Title: The Korean economy : from growth to maturity / by You-il Lee and
Richard Lee.
Description: Abingdon, Oxon ; New York, NY : Routledge, 2019. |
Series: Routledge studies in the modern world economy |
Includes bibliographical references and index.
Identifiers: LCCN 2019004449| ISBN 9781138563896 (hardback) |
ISBN 9781315122038 (ebook)
Subjects: LCSH: Economic development--Korea (South) |
Korea (South)--Economic conditions--2002- |
Korea (South)--Economic policy--2002-
Classification: LCC HC467.965 .L445 2019 | DDC 330.95195--dc23
LC record available at https://lccn.loc.gov/2019004449

ISBN: 978-1-138-56389-6 (hbk)
ISBN: 978-1-03-209274-4 (pbk)
ISBN: 978-1-315-12203-8 (ebk)

Typeset in Galliard
by Taylor & Francis Books

Contents

Illustrations

Figures

Tables

Preface

As the fourth largest economy in Asia and the eleventh largest in the world currently, Korea's economy has developed at an outstanding rate. The nation recorded an average annual economic growth of over 8 per cent between the 1960s and 1990s. In this period, per capita gross national product (GNP) had increased from a meagre USD 80 (1960) to USD 10,500 (1999), with real GNP growth since 1960 expanding by an average of 8 per cent per annum. Within the next two decades, by 2017, Korea's per capita income had nearly topped USD 30,000. As the fifth largest exporter in the world, Korea's trade volume exceeded USD 1 trillion in 2017. These milestones have transformed the image of Korea from that of a primarily agrarian country and a historical recipient of ODA (official development assistance) up until 1995, to that of a newly industrialized country (NIC) based on manufacturing and services in the 1990s. Instead of being on the receiving end, Korea is now the twenty-fourth member of the OECD's international donor's club, the Development Assistance Committee.

This spectacular growth would not have been possible without the government's political economic policies that have supported the phenomenal escalation of foreign direct investments, and hence globalization, in the nation since the early 2000s. Since President Kim Dae-jung's administration (1998–2003), the nation has undergone a new and radical shift by replacing the old model of a developmental state with a new market-oriented paradigm. However, as Korea further sharpens its competitive edge, and as global competition among nations intensifies, it remains to be seen how Korea will continue to evolve its political economic policies, especially in the face of a resurgent Japan and a more assertive China.

As Korea progresses, the evolution of the country's brand image as a nation runs parallel to the development and consequences of Korea's economy policies. While a nation's brand image may not result from any conscious actions by a nation or its people, more often than not, governments make a concerted effort, and are instrumental, in positively shaping this image, especially in view of their international engagements. For Korea, nation branding can be traced back to efforts by its then leader, General Park Chung-hee, shortly following the Korean War (1950–1953), in early attempts to kick start the development of Korea into a globally competitive capitalist economy. Successive governments have continued the legacy of modernizing Korea's brand image, including the formation of the National Image Committee during the administration of President Kim Dae-jung (1998–2003), as well as President Kim Young-Sam's 1993 reformation policy of *segyehwa* (세계화), which institutionalized the link between Korea's economic liberalization and cultural identity. However, as successive governments gained awareness of the critical link between Korea's nation image and its economic development, it has also become clear to them that much work is still needed to advance a positive image of the nation to the world.

Against this backdrop, this book offers detailed insights into the continually changing political, economic and market environments of Korea. Three key areas of the Korean economy over the last five decades are examined, namely the evolution of the Korean political economy, the competitive transition of the Korean political economy, and the maturing economy of Korea particularly from a nation branding perspective. While this book has deviated from conventional economic and market approaches, it offers a cohesive exploration of the political economic framework, which comprises a detailed appraisal of the social, political, cultural and institutional changes reflected in the course of Korea's globalization. A key feature of the book is that the authors also take an in-depth, amalgamated look based on qualitative insights (economic, socio-cultural and political economic analysis) from one-on-one interviews, conducted between 2010 and 2015, with over 40 multinational corporations in Korea as well as with indigenous companies and state actors. Critical insights into these results have not only enriched existing knowledge of the Korean political economy, but they also equally apply to other economies treading a similar globalization path.

You-il Lee and Richard Lee January 2019

Acknowledgements

This work was supported in part by the Seed Program for Korean Studies through the Ministry of Education of the Republic of Korea and the Korean Studies Promotion Service (KSPS) of the Academy of Korean Studies (AKS-2017-INC-2230006). We also acknowledge the financial support for the field trip to Korea conducted in 2015 (AKS-2014-R-01) and the editorial assistance (AKS-2018-P05) provided by the Academy of Korean Studies Grant.

Abbreviations

ADB	Asian Development Bank
AFTA	ASEAN Free Trade Area
AMCHAM	American Chamber of Commerce
ASEAN	Association of South East Asian Nations
BRICS	Brazil, Russia, India, China and South Africa
CEO	Chief Executive Officer
DAC	Development Assistance Committee
DJ	Former president Kim Dae-jung (Korea)
EFTA	European Free Trade Association
EN	Economic Nationalism
EOI	Export-oriented Industrialization
EU	European Union
EUCCK	European Union Chamber of Commerce in Korea
FDI	Foreign Direct Investment
FTA	Free Trade Agreement
FIPA	Foreign Investment Promotion Act
GATT	General Agreement on Tariffs and Trade
GDP	Gross Domestic Product
GNP	Gross National Product
GSCI	Global Sustainable Competitive Index
HCI	Heavy and Chemical Industries
IMF	International Monetary Fund
IFDI	Inward Foreign Direct Investment
ISI	Import Substitution Industrialization
KCC	Kimberly-Clark Corporation
KORUS FTA	Korea-US Free Trade Agreement
KOTRA	Korea Trade-Investment Promotion Agency
KTO	Korea Tourist Organization
LCD	Liquid Crystal Display
M&A	Mergers and Acquisition
MNC	Multinational Corporation
MOFAT	Ministry of Foreign Affairs and Trade
MSIP	Ministry of Science, ICT and Future Planning

NAFTA	North American Free Trade Agreement
NIC	Newly Industrializing Country
ODA	Official Development Assistance
OECD	Organization for Economic Cooperation and Development
OEM	Original Equipment Manufacturer
R&D	Research and Development
RCEP	Regional Comprehensive Economic Partnership
ROI	Return of Investment
RTA	Regional Trade Agreement
SEZ	Special Economic Zones
THAAD	Terminal High Altitude Area Defence
TPP	Trans-Pacific Partnership
TRIPS	Trade-Related Aspects of Intellectual Property Rights
TSS	Trilateral Summit Meeting
UK	United Kingdom
UNCTAD	United Nations Conference on Trade and Development
UNDP	United Nations Development Program
USA	United States of America
USD	US Dollar
WTO	World Trade Organization

1 Introduction

Why Korea?

Within approximately a single generation, South Korea,[1] the Miracle on the Han River, has transformed itself from an aid-dependent developing country following the Korean War,[2] to one of the richest countries in the world. From being a basket-case economy that relied on foreign aid for survival, it is now a donor country that is pulling its weight as a global citizen. Although the 1997 Asian financial crisis threatened to engulf the country's economy, by 2016 Korea emerged as the eleventh largest economy in the world and fourth in Asia after China, Japan and India, according to The World Bank (2017).

A key driver behind this spectacular growth is Korea's political economic policies that support the phenomenal escalation of international capital investment and globalization in Korea since the early 2000s. Following the inception of former Kim Dae-jung administration's (1998–2003) vision of transforming the nation into a Northeast Asian business hub, Korea's industrial development paradigm has undergone a new and radical shift in the economic and business spheres, particularly with a new market-oriented paradigm replacing the old model of a developmental state. The combination of sweeping liberalization measures and pro-foreign direct investment (FDI) institutional reforms enabled Korea to record a dramatic increase in inward FDI since the late 1990s. In 1997, the number of FDIs into Korea was less than 2,000, but by 2010 these had increased seven-fold to more than 14,000.

A salient feature that characterizes Korea's inward FDI-led globalization process is that it was not until 1998, when the Korean National Assembly promulgated the Foreign Investment Promotion Act, that Korea embarked on a path of non-discriminatory treatment of foreign firms. Indeed, the passing of FDI-friendly legislation was an epochal achievement in view of the fact that Korea had rigidly adhered to trade protectionism and a regulation-prone investment regime until the onset of the financial crisis of 1997. However, a closer look at the evolution of the Korean political economy from its first adoption of industrial capitalism to the Kim Dae-jung regime's (1998–2003) first attempt to move the Korean economy from a neo-mercantilist and developmental statist growth model (Korea Inc) of state-capital collusion to one more consistent with the neo-liberal formula of economic globalization embedded in pro-inward FDI policies, reveals that despite some recent efforts by the Korean government to further an economic globalization agenda, a strong and extensive tradition of the collective nature of economic nationalism (i.e. market access barriers in the form of regulations/rules against foreign businesses in Korea) mobilized by the state is still evident in Korea. In other words, Korea's economic growth trajectory has not shifted in the course of Korea's neo-liberal economic trajectory adopted from the late 1990s onwards. As we discuss in Chapter 3 of this book, the collective nature of economic nationalism mobilized by the state is still prevalent in Korea. Despite this radical and relatively sudden change in Korea's economic policy towards FDI, little discussion is available in the literature and public domain on the sustainability of Korea's economic growth, particularly from the viewpoints of the role of foreign companies, the relationship between the *Chaebol* and the multinational corporations (MNCs), and the role of the state in Korea's new economic trajectory.

As Korea progresses economically, the evolution of the country's brand image as a nation runs parallel to the development and consequences of Korea's economic policies. While a nation's brand image can result independently of any conscious actions by the nation or its people, more often than not, governments make concerted efforts to positively shape this image, especially in view of their international engagements. Indeed, Anholt (2008: 23, emphasis in original) has asserted that nation branding is necessarily 'a *component of national policy*, never a "campaign" that is separate from planning, governance, or economic development'. For Korea, nation branding can be traced back to efforts by then leader, General Park Chung-hee, shortly following the Korean War (1950–1953), in early attempts to kick start the development of Korea into a globally competitive capitalist economy. Successive governments have continued the legacy of modernizing Korea's brand image, including the formation of the National Image Committee during the administration of President Kim Dae-jung (1998–2003), as well as President Kim Young-Sam's 1993 reformation policy of *segyehwa* (세계화), which institutionalized the link between Korea's economic liberalization and cultural identity.

However, as successive governments gained awareness of the critical link between Korea's nation image and its economic development, it also became clear to them that much work was still needed to promote a positive image of the nation to the world. Acknowledging that Korea is disadvantaged economically as well as in global politics because of an unfavourable nation brand image, President Lee Myeong-bak formed the Presidential Council on Nation Branding (대통령기록) in 2009 to spearhead and coordinate all nation-branding initiatives by public and private enterprises. Ostensibly, the primary goal of the Council is to raise Korea's stature by gaining credibility and likeability on the global stage by contributing to the international community and helping Koreans become responsible global citizens. However, the government is highly cognisant of the inextricable link between the nation's image and its economy.

One can therefore conclude that whatever dominant shape Korea's competitiveness may take in the future to be successfully integrated into the global economy, will depend not only on the domestic industries and economic policies, but also to what extent the country will be able to portray a favourable nation brand image that can sustain, or even boost, its global competitiveness.

The focus of this book

Against this backdrop, this book takes an in-depth, amalgamated look, from both empirical and qualitative perspectives, into the evolution of the Korean political economy and its nation brand image, particularly from the early 2000s from the Kim Dae-jung (1998–2003), Roh Moo-hyun (2003–2008), Lee Myung-bak (2008–2013), Park Geun-hye (2008-May 2017) to the recently embarked Moon Jae-in administration (May 2017 onwards). During the 1970s and 1980s, Korea achieved the most spectacular economic growth among the developing countries. Yet, in the latter part of 1997, with the onset of the Asian financial crisis, Korea became the first country to receive what was then a record-breaking rescue package from the IMF to prop up its ailing economy. It was obvious that Korea's state-led growth model, embedded in developmental leadership, faced the headwinds brought about by the unavoidable force of free market-driven globalization (IMF). These factors have resulted in the Korean government's dramatic shift towards a neo-liberal FDI and FTA oriented international trade model (i.e. FTA and international business hub). This impressive and positive portrayal of Korea's openness to trade and FDI in the aftermath of the financial crisis should not, however, mislead readers by disguising the fact that Korea's reform measures have not proceeded smoothly, due to the painful and difficult decisions that must be made along the road towards conforming to global standards.

This book provides an overview of Korea's recent economic development in a historical context and offers an analysis of the social relations (political and institutional) that have successfully driven Korea's rapid economic growth in a relatively short period of industrialization. It offers a discourse on the evolution of Korea's economic success through three phases. During the first phase, from the 1960s to 1997, the state enacted policies to propel trade development towards export-oriented industrialization (EOI). The neo-liberal, market-oriented focus in the second phase saw the government facilitating inflows of foreign direct investment and regional integration through free trade agreements. This phase started in the late 1990s and further expanded Korea's trade with its international counterparts, despite setbacks caused by the Asian financial crisis in 1997. Finally, the third phase saw Korea's journey to become a modern-day high-tech powerhouse. The book also chronicles the evolution of Korea's nation brand image from its days as a backwater and low value-adding manufacturer to becoming a modern and industrialized nation whose exports include not only its well-known consumer electronic products but also its distinctive culture commonly known as Korean Wave or the *Hanryu* (한류) neologism of K-pop, K-drama and K-beauty. Finally, the book offers insights into the existence and prevalence of nationalism among Korean consumers.

As Korea looks to the next decade and beyond, the country will continue to grapple with the challenges of assuring and sustaining buoyant economic growth, consumer welfare gains and job creation by expanding trade and investment, as well as maintaining or even improving its nation brand image in the face of increasing competition globally. Moreover, there are rising threats from a resurgent Japan, Korea's inability to compete with China on a large scale and a menacing northern neighbour. Korea wants its international standing to be commensurate with the economic success it has built since 1960s. Hence, as Korea looks to the next decade and beyond, whatever dominant shape Korea's competitiveness and its high-tech nation brand image will take in the future will depend on the industries the country is able to develop and sustain competitively during its fourth industrial revolution in the face of global competition.

Structure of this book

In addition to this introductory Chapter 1 and the concluding Chapter 7, this book consists of three main parts with a total of six chapters. Part I (Chapter 2) is dedicated to enriching existing knowledge on the evolution of the Korean political economy from the early period of industrialization (1960s) to the period of Korea's globalization drive spearheaded by Kim Dae-jung (1998–2003), Roh Moo-hyun (2003–2008), Lee Myung-bak (2008–2013) and Park Geun-hye (2013-May 2017) and Moon Jae-in (May 2017 to present). This part offers a detailed analysis of the changing Korean market/business environment triggered by the IMF rescue package and of socio-political and cultural aspects of the Korean business culture as well as prospects and dilemmas in the Korean economy.

Part I also details the legacy of Korea's state-led capitalism, which is arguably very much entrenched in the Korean economy and plays a major role in deterring Korea's new economic vision. Various economic agendas adopted from the Kim Dae-jung to the Park Geun-hye regimes during the process of globalization, whether neoliberal or neo-mercantilist, have been found to be subordinate to the goal of state building and safeguarding the interests of the state. Part I also explores whether Korea's long-standing tradition of neo-mercantilism remains an appropriate development strategy or whether this approach has been rendered irrelevant by the wave of MNC-led neoliberal globalization since the early 2000s with particular focus on national identity and economic nationalism, mobilized and implemented by the state.

The second part of the book (Chapter 3) reviews and uncovers the current market environment in Korea from 1998 to 2018. It offers a comparative analysis of the changing nature of economic and policy agendas, Korean business culture and business environment from the Kim Dae-jung to the Park Geun-hye and the Moon regimes. In particular, this part examines the fundamental question of whether the new Korean market environment in terms of international business, has been created, shaped and sustained by the advent of Korea's entry into the global economy as a capital importer since the early 2000s.

A key feature of Part II is the data on multinational corporations' (MNCs) perceptions of Korea's new economic trajectory, Korea's capabilities to attract foreign R&D centres and the forces driving MNC investments. The data was collected from fieldwork performed in Korea over the past decade. Specifically, an analysis of in-depth interviews with 49 Korea-based MNC executives, conducted between April and September 2010 and some of revisits in 2015, was made with the aim of shedding light on the factors that have affected decisions to establish R&D centres in Korea and/or to set future investment directions. The interviewees include the CEOs of foreign investment companies (R&D-driven) and the chairmen of foreign chambers of commerce in Korea. These new insights highlight the challenges to the Korean government's FDI-driven globalization and its newly-established vision of transforming the nation into a Northeast Asian business hub, initiated by the Kim Dae-jung administration.

Part III of this book focuses on the branding of Korea as a nation, and the impacts of the nation brand image on its culture, economy and products. Chapters 4 to 6 in this part are organized as follows. Chapter 4 discusses the development of 'Korea' as a brand, a concept commonly referred to as nation branding (Anholt, 2005; Dinnie, 2016). Parallel to the discussion on the development of 'brand Korea', Chapter 5 traces the development of post-war industrialization in Korea, and how it transformed the nation brand image of Korea from a backwater developing country to a twenty-first century economic and high-technology powerhouse. Having covered the issues of Korea's nation brand at a macro-level in the first two chapters, Chapter 6 highlights the impacts of country-of-origin, as a dimension of Korea's nation brand, on Korean products. The chapter also studies the behaviour of Korean consumers by relating their consumption behaviour to their nationalistic dispositions.

Finally, the concluding chapter, Chapter 7, summarizes and crystallizes the significance of the issues discussed across the earlier chapters, offers constructive recommendations on critical challenges that Korea faces today in developing and integrating itself into the international economy and provides insights into the future of 'brand Korea' in the next decade and beyond. It discusses policy issues as well as socio-political and cultural dilemmas that Korea faces in sustaining the country's economic competitiveness.

Notes

1 South Korea, or more formally the Republic of Korea, is referred to as Korea throughout this book, unless otherwise specifically mentioned.
2 From 1910–1945 the Korean peninsula was part of the Japanese Empire. After its independence from Japan in 1945, the United States and the Soviet Union split the country. The ensuing Korean War (1950–1953) ended in stalemate and resulted in the country being delineated along the 38th parallel. Since then the two Koreas, The Democratic People's Republic of Korea (North) and the Republic of Korea (South), have officially remained enemies.

Part I
The political economy of Korea

2 The evolution of the Korean political economy

Korea's phenomenal economic success post-World War II is a well-known story. Over the past four decades, Korea has transformed itself from an agricultural nation to a high-tech powerhouse. In 2017, a rebound in business investment and the continued strength of residential investment increased output growth to 3.1 per cent. Private consumption strengthened while employment growth slowed markedly in the first quarter of 2018. The tightening of loan-to-value and debt-to-income regulation on mortgage lending has reduced the rise in residential property construction orders from a peak of 76 per cent (year-on-year) to below 2 per cent. Its economic growth in 2019 is projected to remain around 3 per cent, supported by stronger export growth and fiscal stimulus that offset the impact of tighter regulations on housing and mortgage lending, which will slow construction investment. Inflation is projected to rise toward the 2 per cent target, while the current account surplus is likely to narrow to around 4 per cent of Gross Domestic Product (GDP) (OECD, 2018).

Historically, the Korean people have lived under the authoritarian rule of government for many centuries. It is generally considered that the authoritarian regimes in Korea were quite successful (Kwon, 2010). The regimes were committed to economic development without serious predatory activities. They established proper institutions for secured property rights and market competition, and established policy-making organizations staffed with efficient officials. Economic policies met the success criteria of decisiveness, consistency, credibility and long-term orientation. The military regimes also met the criterion of encompassing interests of the general public, excluding special-interest organizations and including unions which remained repressed. In the last decades of the twentieth century, the new notions of democracy and prosperity arose to capture the national imagination and to become the primary concern of the government leadership. The idea of modernization inspired the soldiers turned-politicians during the authoritarian phase of Korean politics in the 1970s to initiate a program of socioeconomic development through industrialization. The democratic movement launched in the early 1960s, and then by opposition leaders in the 1970s, came to fruition in Korean politics in the late 1980s. In 1987, the Korean political system made a historic transition from authoritarianism to democracy and held the first free and competitive presidential election. Subsequently, with the inauguration of

Kim Dae-jung as president in 1998, Korea officially entered an era of consolidated democracy.

Economically, one of the most spectacular phenomena in the Korean political economy in the twentieth century has been the phenomenal escalation of international capital investment or globalization in Korea since the early 2000s. With the arrival of the Kim Dae-jung administration (1998–2003) and its vision of transforming the nation into a Northeast Asian business hub, Korea's industrial development paradigm has undergone a new and radical shift in the economic and business spheres, particularly towards a new market-oriented paradigm in place of the old model of a developmental state. The combination of sweeping liberalization measures and pro-foreign direct investment (FDI) institutional reforms enabled Korea to record a dramatic increase in inward FDI since the late 1990s (Kim and Lee, 2007). This radical change was marked by a substantial opening of the domestic market to foreign capital and seemingly favourable attitudes towards foreign capital in the state's strategic policy direction under the banner of globalization, thus tracing Korea's new economic trajectory since the 2000s.

Against this backdrop, this chapter provides an overview of Korea's economic development in a historical context and offers an analysis of the social, political and institutional relations that have driven Korea's rapid economic growth in a relatively short period of industrialization. The chapter takes an in-depth, amalgamated look into the evolution of the Korean political economy from Korea's early state-led international trade development characterized by export-oriented industrialization and EOI, between the 1960s and 1990s, and the recent phase of neoliberal/market oriented international trade development based on inflow of foreign direct investment and regional economic integration through free trade agreements. The latter strategy was initiated by the Kim Dae-jung (1998–2003) administration and continued through to the Roh Moo-hyun (2003–2008), Lee Myung-bak (2008–2013), Park Geun-hye (2008- May 2017) regimes, as well as the recently embarked Moon Jae-in administration (May 2017 onwards).

First phase of industrialization: 1960s–1997

Korea's industrialization, late particularly by Western timelines, kick started in earnest in the early 1960s, joined by the formation of the *Chaebol*, [1] to spearhead large scale export-oriented industrialization. According to a recent report by Deloitte (GMCI 2016), Korea's manufacturing industry accounted for about 86 per cent of total merchandise exports. The country has come a long way since the post-Korean War (1950–1953) period when manufacturing accounted for a mere 12 per cent of gross domestic product (GDP) which increased to about 30 per cent in 2017. However, industrialization objectives and characteristics, articulated in successive five-year plans under different administrations, differed vastly from early post-war days through to recent times.

Korea was predominantly an agricultural economy up until the Korean War. During the early 1960s, the government's import substitution industrialization (ISI) policies were aimed at making Koreans self-reliant while increasing their wealth (Chung, 1974), although some have argued that the approach was a mistake (see Harvie and Lee, 2003). Korea chose this policy (EOI) due to various unfavourable national conditions for economic development such as limited natural resources, negligible domestic savings and the lack of development experience. The change of economic policy from ISI to EOI involved a revaluation of the currency (about 12 per cent) in 1964 and the establishment of a Free Export Zone for industries such as electronics and motor vehicles.

Economic conditions in Korea in the 1960s were similar to those of most resource-poor, low-income, developing countries. Population was growing at an annual rate of 2.9 per cent and there was widespread unemployment. The 1962 per capita gross national product (GNP) in current prices was only USD 120, and the level of domestic savings was negligible. The nation had no significant exports, which amounted to only USD 54 million, and had run chronic balance of payments deficits ever since the establishment of an independent government in 1948. By implementing successive five-year plans, the Korean government systemically enacted import substitution policies through tariffs and subsidies, as well as through regulations and restrictions on foreign investments and technology transfers in order to develop strong local companies that were capable of competing internationally. The omnipresence of the state in guiding or even regulating private industries benefitted major family-owned *Chaebol* as major financial resources and coveted public infrastructure projects were channelled to them. In turn, the *Chaebol* invested heavily in R&D that would eventually result in world-class brands including the likes of Samsung and Hyundai (Shin, 2005). The characteristics of the country's industrialization process have long been considered to be underpinned by political nationalism.

Some credit for the rapid success of Korea's industrialization should also be attributed to the government's development of special economic zones (SEZ) starting from the 1970s. These zones served to attract foreign investments through policies favouring a one-stop-shop processing of import/export customs procedures, and financial incentives offering cheaper access to land for rental, in order to enhance the competitiveness of Korean exports (Jeong and Pek, 2016). Among these measures, the Masan Export Processing Zone (later renamed as Masan Free Trade Zone) was the first designated bonded processing zone. Consequently, many prominent multinational corporations, such as Nokia, Sony, Sanyo and Matsushita, set up businesses within the zone. This not only formed a concentrated cluster that synergized the development of support businesses by Korean companies, it also facilitated the transfer of advanced technologies and business know-how that would later feed the competitiveness and growth of Korean businesses.

Second phase of industrialization: globalization

Korea's remarkable economic achievement during the first phase of industrialization was not free of problems. Korea faced many of the uncertainties that had been triggered by the so-called economic miracle in the 1980s. For example, since the mid-1980s, the country had been confronted by a variety of issues; these included the emergence of new protectionism from the advanced industrial countries, particularly from the United States and the European Union, and looming competition from the newly emerging economic superstars of Southeast Asia such as Indonesia, Thailand and Malaysia. At home, Korea also had to contend with other challenges, such as the increasing social and political tensions such as labour and management conflicts, the growing discrepancy between the 'haves' and 'have-nots'. Moreover, there were worsening infrastructural imbalances in the economy, particularly in the high-tech industries, where there was an under-development of small and medium-sized firms.

With rising labour costs since 1987, Korean industries and the economy had, to some extent, lost their competitive lustre in the global market as a manufacturing base. While during the 1970s and 1980s, Korea had achieved the most spectacular economic growth among developing countries, in the latter part of 1990s, Korea became the first country among the 'East-Asian Tigers' to receive what was a record-breaking USD 58 billion rescue package from the International Monetary Fund (IMF) to remedy its ailing economy as a result of the so-called '1997 Asian Financial Crisis'. This marked the end of the country's long-hailed reputation as a newly industrialized country and even as an advanced industrial country.

As briefly discussed above, two distinct schools of thought (neo-classical and statist) on Korea's rapid growth have their own unique explanations. While the neo-classical school treats Korea's success as a classic economic model that shows the virtues of the Western capitalist system, the statists or institutionalists see a different paradigm from that of the Western perspective, and that difference is the key to Korea's economic triumph (Frankel, 1998). However, this school of thought does not explain the crisis during the second phase given that Korea's economic success had been rooted either in the nation's adherence to the market principles and minimal state intervention or so-called western capitalism or in the strong capacity of the state. Nor does this view explain why the Korean economy was collapsing under such circumstances.

Economists tend to contribute various macroeconomic (capital inflows, real exchange rate application) and microeconomic (credit expansion, financial regulation and supervision) factors to the Asian Financial crisis (Radelet and Sachs, 1998). Corsetti, Pesenti and Roubini (1998) suggest that the cause of the crisis is rooted in the inconsistency of policies aimed at simultaneously sustaining growth, investment and risk-taking, as well as maintaining stable exchange rates and providing guarantees to under-regulated financial institutions. In the absence of fully developed and sophisticated securities markets, these policies caused large account imbalances. Similarly, Krugman (1998) suggests that the Asian financial crisis might have been only incidentally about currencies, but it was mainly about bad banking and its consequences. Krugman indicates a problem of 'moral hazard asset bubble', which created severe inflation–not of goods but of asset prices such as land and stock–as a major contender for a leading role in the crisis (Krugman, 1998). On the contrary, unlike the neo-classical economists, state-centred theorists see the problems and causes in relation to capacity of the developmental state. Weiss and Hobson (1998), for example, argue that the Asian financial crisis is fundamentally rooted in the vulnerability of government capacity to strong winds of global finance.

One of the seemingly most painful IMF conditions for Korea was the requirement to open its industry to foreign competition, including foreign investment reforms in financial services and trade reform and liberalization.[2] As indicated earlier, Korea's economic policies used to be state-*Chaebol*-driven, with a strong protectionist approach to foreign competition in the local market. To turn the distorted Korean economy into a healthy economy, the new government under Kim Dae-jung (DJ) (1998–2003) had shown a strong commitment to the priorities and steps prescribed by the IMF to be taken by restructuring the financial sectors, mostly banks and the *Chaebol*. Ironically though, the financial crisis coupled with externally driven pressures imposed by the IMF rescue package provided opportunities to implement major reforms, including hostile mergers and acquisitions (M&As), full opening of the domestic market to foreign products and massive restructuring of financial institutions and, more importantly, large corporate groups or the *Chaebol*.

Globalization

The currency crisis and its serious impact on the Korean economy resulted in a noticeable shift in Korea's attitude towards foreign companies and products. Firstly, in an effort to restore the distorted Korean economy to a healthy state, the DJ administration showed strong commitment by implementing decisive reforms in certain sectors, in particular with regard to financial and corporate (*Chaebol*) restructuring. The aim was to eliminate Korea's chronic condition caused by the tight government-business collusion, to enhance transparency and supervision, and to restore market confidence. Considering the currency meltdown, it was generally accepted by the DJ administration and the Korean people that foreign capital was critical to remedy the ailing economy. Not only did foreign direct investment in Korea stabilize the foreign exchange market but also it eventually helped in restructuring the economy and increasing economic efficiency. The Foreign Investment Promotion Act of November 1998 abolished restrictions on the foreign ownership of land and hostile cross-border mergers and acquisitions (M&As) and allowed foreign participation in large public enterprises and key industries (EAAU, 1999). This draconian change in the government's policy in favour of inbound investments shifted the Korean economy toward a market oriented neoclassical economic growth paradigm based on inward FDI and replaced the old model of the state-led development strategy.

Under the guidance of the IMF from early 1998, the Korean economy rebounded from its late 1997 meltdown faster than expected. After falling by nearly 7 per cent in 1998, real GDP was almost 11 per cent in 1999 and near 9 per cent in 2000. Following the opening of its market to outside players, international capital flows into Korea rose from a meagre USD 27.4 million in 1987 to more than USD 32 billion in 1996 (Economist Intelligence Unit, 2002). Since the early 1990s, the affiliates of more than 16,000 foreign multinational corporations (MNCs) have established operations in fields ranging from consumer products to high-tech industries operating in Korea. In addition to IMF-mandated structural reforms, a lower value of the local currency (won), declining status of the *Chaebol*, and the government's strong push for investment liberalization measures, there was an upsurge of FDI inflows into Korea (Chang, 1998; Weiss and Hobson, 1998; Kim and Rowley, 2001; Noland, 2005b; Shin, 2005). While the amount of total inward FDI during the period from 1962 to 1997 was minimal, total FDI during the eight-year period from 1998 to 2005 alone tallied about USD 91 billion on a notification basis, which is nearly quadruple the USD 25 billion posted during the previous 35 years, or about 79 per cent of the USD 115 billion aggregate FDI figure recorded from 1962 to 2005 (Ministry of Commerce, Industry and Energy, 2007).

Korea has also been very determined since the 1997 Asian financial crisis to become a regional Free Trade Agreement (FTA)[3] hub nation in order to overcome its relatively small domestic market and participate actively in a rapidly regionalized world. In fact, until its first FTA with Chile in 2004, Korea had established no bilateral trade agreements, nor did it have any plan for FTAs with foreign countries. The 1997 Asian financial crisis that hit Korea hard was a key triggering factor behind Korea's aggressive pursuit for FTAs as a matter of survival. As discussed earlier, the major structural reforms mandated by the IMF consisted of restructuring troubled financial institutions, improving corporate governance and enhancing labour market flexibility. The IMF also demanded equally important external reforms. One of the top economic policy priorities of the DJ administration centred on engaging with foreign companies to attract foreign direct investment (FDI) into Korea. In terms of trade liberalization, the DJ administration launched a series of FTA negotiations in 1998 with the aim of overcoming the currency crisis, strengthening the competitiveness of Korean industry and boosting exports (Ye, 2017).

Dramatically, the late 1990s saw the sudden emergence of Korea as a major recipient of foreign capital for both strategic and non-strategic industrial areas, ranging from consumer products (e.g. alcohol, tobacco, cosmetics and textiles) to telecommunications. As a consequence, the 1990s witnessed a flood of foreign products as well as an increasing number of foreign multinational corporations (MNCs) operating in Korea. Since Korea's financial crisis, more than 1,500 MNCs have established operations in Korea in fields ranging from consumer products to high-tech industries. This trend implies that the Korean market is rapidly changing and is open to outsiders offering opportunities to maximize market benefits. This feature is one of the most revolutionary of the Korean economy in the twentieth century, contrasting with the previous four decades of the Korean political economy. Many neo-liberal supporters, such as international financial institutions, described Korea's 'economic recovery and financial stabilization' as remarkable (Crotty and Lee, 2001). Consequently, the IMF loans were paid off by mid-2001. In terms of regional integration strategy, as of January 2017, Korea had concluded 15 FTAs with 52 countries, namely with ASEAN (Association of Southeast Asian Countries, ten countries), Australia, Canada, Chile, China, Colombia, EFTA (European Free Trade Association, four countries), the EU (European Union, twenty-eight countries), India, New Zealand, Peru, Turkey and the USA.

However, the role of FDI and FTAs throughout Korea's legacy of economic development has been insignificant to say the least. In fact, the level of FDI/FTAs relative to the size of the economy had been quite negligible when compared to that of other countries in East Asia. This fact can be verified by a number of indicators. According to the World Investment Report of the United Nations Conference on Trade and Development (UNCTAD, 2006), the inward FDI stock in Korea as a percentage of current GDP in 2005 was 8.0 per cent, above Japan (2.2 per cent) but below the levels of Taiwan (12.1 per cent), China (14.3 per cent), and Singapore (15.8 per cent). What then has accounted for the relatively minor role played by FDI/FTAs in Korea's economic development in comparison with its Asian neighbours? In the initial period of Korea's modern economic growth during the 1960s, the inflow of foreign capital was encouraged to make up for the shortage of domestic savings and foreign reserves. However, the Korean government preferred foreign borrowing over FDI, since this allowed it to control foreign resources. The general fear of Korean industries being dominated by foreign entities was deeply rooted in Korea's then recent history of Japanese colonization from 1910 to 1945 and was too widespread for the government to be in a position to accommodate foreign management. Even today there is a lingering suspicion that FDI/FTAs are just a conduit through which foreigners and foreign countries attempt to control Korean industries. While Korean leaders today show preferences towards FTAs, they face strong domestic interest groups and opposition (Ye 2017:152). However, undoubtedly Korea has emerged in recent decades as one of the most active states in attracting FDI and pursuing FTAs with partners across the globe. Ravenhill (2003) points to three factors to explain the prevalent trend toward bilateral FTAs: (1) an increasing awareness of the weakness of existing regional institutions and initiatives; (2) perceptions of positive demonstration effects from regional agreements in other parts of the world; and (3) changing domestic economic interests after the economic crisis.

Financial crisis and the Kim Dea-jung administration (1998–2003)

After losing three elections in 1971, 1987 and 1992, Kim Dae-jung finally won the presidential election in 1997. His victory signified monumental progress as it was the first peaceful leadership transition to an opposition candidate through a free and fair election; it also ended almost four decades of conservative rule. Being the first progressive president elected since the 1987 constitutional reform, his major policy agendas included salvaging the failing national economy from the impact of the previous government's actions, unifying a Korean society that had been polarized by region and ideology, terminating the Cold War legacy and building peace on the Korean Peninsula (Woo, 2017). This section will examine three of the important policy priories of the Kim Dae-jung administration: economic reform, the Sunshine Policy and national reconciliation.

The 1997 financial crisis revealed that the country could no longer sustain the developmental state model of the economy in which the government had played a dominant role in economic policy making and implementation. President Kim described the financial crisis as 'the greatest national crisis since the Korean War' and declared that no solution could be found to deal with the financial crisis without fundamental reforms.

The Kim government's reform was initiated by the cosy relationship between the government and big businesses especially the *Chaebol*. The *Chaebol* had received preferential benefits with generous policy loans, tax breaks and other favours at the expense of small and medium-sized businesses, urban workers and farmers (Kim, 2001). In particular, a small number of *Chaebol* were the beneficiaries of considerable favouritism, which disadvantaged other market participants, creating a highly corrupt, inefficient and backward market (Kang, 2002). Ironically, the Kim government itself was the main source of corruption, as Kim's second son and other close political aides were convicted of exerting influence and accepting bribes. With the failure of domestically-driven reform, Korea had to accept the restructuring plan put forward by the International Monetary Fund (IMF). The IMF demanded extensive structural reforms, including budget cuts, higher tax rates, the opening up of financial markets to foreigners, the restructuring of the *Chaebol* and increased transparent government-business relations (Park, 1999). The IMF restructuring plan was painful to Koreans and provoked socio-political conflicts among key stakeholders including bureaucrats, the *Chaebol* and workers over who should be held responsible for the economic recession and who would take on the burden of restructuring. On the one hand, nationwide grassroots movements were initiated to rescue the economy. Approximately 3.5 million citizens voluntarily donated 227 tons of gold to help the nation's foreign debt, cut their consumption, saved more and bought products made in Korea (Pollack, 1997). The situation presented the opportunity for a complete overhaul of the *Chaebol*-dominated economy in Korea. On the other hand, intense political fighting took place as the business sector blamed the militant labour unions and workers criticized the *Chaebol*'s unprincipled management and corrupted ties with government.

Since the IMF plan focused on reforming the *Chaebol*, the financial, public and labour sectors, the labour-business-government commission was launched. This commission aimed to dismantle corrupt ties between the *Chaebol* and government, and to scale down the *Chaebol*'s dominance over Korea's economy. For the first time in modern Korea, the labour sector was recognized as an equal partner with government and business in economic policy making, and labour union rights were recognized. The *Chaebol* had been responsible for mismanagement resulting in a national economic crisis; now fair burden-sharing between business and labour was identified as a means of turning the crisis around. However, when the economy showed signs of recovery, both labour and business sectors became impatient (Kihl, 2005). Labour protested against its unfairly imposed burden of reform, while the business sector wanted freedom from government control. During Kim's presidency, the number of labour strikes rose from 129 in 1999 to 250 in 2003 and the concentration of the economy in the *Chaebol* intensified during the same period (Suh, 2015).

Another critical agenda for the Kim government was to terminate friction between Korea and North Korea. In his inaugural speech, President Kim proclaimed three policy principles in this regard, namely, no tolerance of armed provocation of any kind, no intention to undermine or absorb North Korea, and the active pursuit of reconciliation and cooperation between the two Koreas (Korea and North Korea). He expressed a willingness to expand economic, cultural and academic exchanges, and stressed that he was ready to hold a summit if Pyongyang was amenable to the idea. His Sunshine Policy separated political-military confrontation from economic relations, focused on expanding economic cooperation to rescue poverty-stricken North Korea and build mutual trust between the two Koreas (Moon, 2001). The Sunshine Policy culminated in the historic summit between two Korean governments. The policy produced the North-South Joint Declaration with the agreement to resolve humanitarian issues, such as reunions of separated family members (August 2000 and November 2000), expansion of economic, social and cultural changes, and ultimately Korean reunification. Both governments also agreed to regular and institutionalized meetings (Kihl, 2005). The Sunshine Policy led Kim Dae-jung to win the Nobel Peace Prize in 2000. However, the Sunshine Policy and the North-South reconciliation did not progress further as planned. Abroad, the George W. Bush administration alleged that Pyongyang had been violating the 1994 Agreed Framework by secretly continuing nuclear projects. He called North Korea (with Iran and Iraq) an 'axis of evil' that destabilized international security and promoted global terrorism. In 2003, North Korea declared its withdrawal from the Nuclear Non-proliferation Treaty and reopened the Yongbyon nuclear facilities. Domestically, the Sunshine Policy was challenged for its lack of reciprocity. The conservative opposition utilized the policy as a platform for political attacks on the Kim government and acquired domestic support. Another important agenda of the Kim government was national reconciliation for a country that was ideologically, regionally and economically polarized. By releasing the two former generals-turned-presidents, Kim's symbolic gesture aimed to alleviate regional divisions. However, his efforts towards reconciliation failed.

President Kim Dae-jung was seemingly successful at the beginning of his term in managing the financial crisis and implementing various institutional reforms, largely because the whole nation was united behind him to overcome the devastating crisis. In his final year in office, he admitted that his economic reform policies had not met much success and he apologized for corruption scandals within his political inner circle, including events involving two of his sons. Moreover, his Sunshine Policy was compromised when it was revealed that the Kim government had offered Pyongyang a financial donation in return for holding the North-South summit. Furthermore, his efforts toward national reconciliation, his economic reforms and peace-building with North Korea worsened regional divisions.

Ironically though, the 1997 financial crisis coupled with externally driven pressures imposed by the IMF rescue package offered opportunities for implementing major reforms, including hostile mergers and acquisitions (M&As), full opening of the domestic market to foreign products, and massive restructuring of financial institutions and the *Chaebol*. Only after teetering on the brink of default in late December 1997 during the currency crisis, did Korea realize that short-term borrowing carried substantial hazards and that FDI inflows could act as an important stabilizer against the risk of financial panic. The Korean government's adoption of sweeping measures to actively promote FDI can be best summed up by the enactment of the Foreign Investment Promotion Act (FIPA) of 1998. This landmark piece of legislation guaranteed legally and unconditionally international remittances by foreign investors even under certain circumstances of exogenous shocks such as natural disasters and wars (Article 3). Simply put, the aim of the reforms was to change the engine of the Korean economy from *Chaebol* expansion to inward FDI. As Ha and Lee noted:

> The primary objective of government reform was to transform the state-led economic system into a market-friendly system. To this end, the administration undertook financial liberalization, corporate restructuring, labour market flexibility and privatization.
> (Ha and Lee, 2007)

In contrast to the dwindling FDI outflows, FDI inflows began to surge from 1997 and maintained strong growth until 2002. FDI inflows in 1997 were valued at USD 7 billion, which is more than double the previous year's figure. FDI inflows peaked in 1999 and 2000, reaching USD 15.5 billion (11 per cent of exports) and USD 15.2 billion (8.8 percent of exports), respectively (Min, 2006). Out of a total of 1,148 inward FDI subject sectors, 1,117 sectors were completely opened, and 18 sectors were partially opened to foreign investors at the end of 1998 (Min, 2006).

The Roh Moo-hyun presidency

Roh Moo-hyun won the presidential election in December 2002, receiving support from a younger generation. His presidency ended the old legacy of the three Kims (Kim Young-sam, Kim Dae-jung and Kim Jong-pil). Unlike his predecessors, his presidency began with a much more positive environment; North-South Korea relations had improved after the Sunshine Policy, Korea's economy had recovered from financial crisis and democracy had become further consolidated. The public held high expectations of the Roh presidency, hoping that the government could further advance the democratic process, overcome regional divisions, engage Pyongyang more deeply and continue economic prosperity. Roh proclaimed his regime as a 'participatory democracy' and launched several major policy initiatives in order to carry out reforms and foster national unity (Lee, 2004).

Firstly, he intended to restructure Korea's security alliance with the United States, which had broad implications for the country's political place in East Asia. President Roh was eager to redefine Korea's security policy direction from Washington, seeking a more sovereign foreign policy stance. He repeatedly announced ambitious military modernization programs for the air, sea and land forces in an effort to deter the threat from North Korea. Correspondingly, the Bush government announced that all US troops in the Demilitarized Zone would be relocated and downsized the US military presence in Korea. Such an arrangement was welcomed by the younger generation (born in the 1960s) who were confident in the country's military strength in deterring the threat from North Korea. Young people also supported regaining Wartime Operation Control from the United States. At the same time, the older generation who was more conservative and had experienced the nightmare of the Korean War, fiercely opposed Roh's foreign policy (Cha, 2005).

In terms of domestic politics, the Roh Government enacted four reform laws which included the National Security Law, media law, education law and the Truth and Reconciliation Law. The president and his ruling party pushed for abolishment of National Security Law as the law had been used frequently to curtail freedom of expression and silence dissidents. Receiving fierce opposition from the conservative parties, President Roh failed to abolish the law. Meanwhile, the Truth and Reconciliation Law was passed with the aim of uncovering the truth about pro-Japanese collaborators during the Japanese occupation as well as injustices committed by the military regimes. The Truth and Reconciliation Commission uncovered more than 200 cases of innocent civilians being killed by US troops during the Korean War. Although justice was served, the investigation ironically polarized the country and was frequently criticized as 'being politically motivated' (Kim, 2011).

A long-time human rights lawyer criticized Roh's administration for 'political amateurism'. Roh's presidency suffered from a lack of presidential power and he was not able to demonstrate any significant accomplishments in economic development as promised. His presidential weakness partially came from his own desire to make his office more democratic by decentralizing political power. With a lack of leadership in his own party and poor coordination skills, his presidential authority was further weakened. After just one year in office, he was impeached by the National Assembly on two counts of illegal campaign funding (Faiola, 2004).

Although public opinion about the Roh government was polarized, he managed to open the Kaesong Industrial Complex and to hold a second North-South summit in 2007. The Industrial Complex was funded by the Korean government and hired more than 50,000 workers from North Korea; it represented the first tangible outcomes of Seoul's effort to engage Pyongyang economically. The Complex effectively reduced military tensions between the two Koreas; however, it immediately met with opposition from the US and the opposition conservatives (Kim and Lie, 2007). Nevertheless, the summit produced several agreements to improve inter-Korean relations including creating a special peace and cooperation zone in the West Sea, expanding the Kaesong Industrial Complex further, reconstructing the railways across the Demilitarized Zone, and opening a direct flight between Seoul and Mount Baekdu, among other initiatives (Oberdorfer and Carlin, 2013).

In terms of economic policies and growth strategy, the Roh Moo-hyun administration inherited Kim Dae-jung's achievements on the external front (opening its markets and implementing sweeping market-oriented reforms). Initially, Roh Moo-hyun offered a glimpse of what Korea could do better externally through his 'globalization efforts' aimed at transforming the nation into a knowledge-based service-oriented economy and enlarging and solidifying the hub vision launched by his predecessor. However, the Roh Moo-hyun regime, which came into power leaning towards egalitarianism, often defied the market dictates and was lukewarm about extending the potential benefits of globalization. Furthermore, under the Roh administration, the National Assembly, the judiciary, the tax authority, several interest groups and the Korean media added fuel to the rise of traditional doctrines of economic nationalism by demonstrating their fear of a growing foreign presence in Korea. In fact, a host of foreign business grievance cases during that period cast serious doubts on the Roh regime's announced commitment to inward FDI liberalization and its adherence to the globalization path (Fairclough, 2005; Graham, 2005). Equally important in consolidating this attitude was the Korean mentality towards and perception of foreign countries and economic globalization. Despite its remarkable economic transformation in the late twentieth century from a predominantly agricultural society into an industrial one, a corresponding change in people's perceptions had not materialized. The continuing rise of sentiment opposed to foreign capital due to the growing presence of foreign-controlled banks, the entry of foreign equity funds and a series of anti-globalization/ liberalism protests in 2009 (against a free trade agreement with the US and imports of American beef), raised the question as to whether Korea was reverting to the Korea of old, that is, to a country dictated by isolationism, self-sufficiency and the closed mindset of the people (Fairclough, 2005; Noland, 2005a). In this sense, Korea's stance toward foreign investment was 'at best ambivalent' (Klingner and Kim, 2007). The significant increase of foreign capital in Korea from the late 1990s has been closely related to the Korean state's change in economic policies, particularly towards foreign capital. These economic activities, whether neo-liberal or neo-mercantilist, adopted over the process of capitalist industrialization during this era of economic globalization, were still found to be subordinate to the goal of state building and the interests of the state. This observation suggests a very different consideration from the tradition of economic liberalism, which emphasizes factor endowments. In fact, this study reveals that the Korean regimes' 'liberal motivation for liberalization' has been directed and promoted by developmental and neo-mercantilist policies. The following comment made by an official of the Korean Ministry of Foreign Affairs and Trade effectively reflected this sentiment: 'Selling Daewoo to Ford, GM or any other foreign companies to many Koreans equates to selling your country' (cited in Dent, 2003). There is, however, a more fundamental issue to be addressed, namely, the concept of globalization as perceived by the three previous regimes of Kim Dae-jung and Roh Moo-hyun. The Kim Dae-jung administration encouraged FDI inflows only to rescue an ailing economy and to promote Korea's competitiveness. In addition, Kim's external reforms aimed at attracting foreign capital by guaranteeing market predictability, financial transparency and a flexible labour market as mandated by the IMF rather than implemented through his own initiative (Cho, 2009). In other words, he did not have a consciously drawn neo-liberal globalization strategy. At most, Kim's globalization efforts took the form of a vision for Korea to become the financial and logistics hub of Northeast Asia; however, he failed to push this vision forward along the road to globalization. As indicated earlier, Korea's economic policies have a history of being state-driven and nationalistic, and Korea, like Japan, has long spurned and minimized foreign competition in the local market. Hence Korea's industrialization strategy has worked only in favour of the *Chaebol*.

The Lee Myung-bak presidency

The failure of two previous presidents to meet the expectations of the majority of Koreans on inter-Korean relations and national economy resulted in the return of conservatism. In this sense, the Lee Myung-bak presidency represented the fall of progressive politics and the rise of conservatism in Korea. Lee Myung-bak won the presidential election through the popularity of the 'lost decade' slogan. Support for the slogan implied that Koreans had not been satisfied with how the national economy had been handled and felt that too much had been given away, while too little had been asked of North Korea (Oberdorfer and Carlin, 2013).

President Lee developed his political image as the mayor of Seoul and an effective leader who carried out projects such as restoring the Chenggycheon[4] (청계천: Cheng (clean, 청) gyechoon (계천: open stream), reformatting Seoul's public transportation system, opening Seoul Forest Park, and hosting the 2002 FIFA World Cup. During his presidential campaign, he proposed the 7–4–7 plan for the national economy, where '7' stood for 7 per cent annual growth in GDP, '4' stood for USD 40,000 GDP per capita, the last '7' stood for elevating Korea to the seventh largest economy in the world by the end of his presidency. Counting on voters' high expectations of the national economy, Lee won with a winning margin of more than 5.2 million votes.

However, Lee's political power evaporated quickly in the first year of his presidency, largely due to new policy directions and his 'entrepreneur-style' leadership which contradicted democratic political procedures. Criticism started when Lee formed his cabinet; for example, the use of sarcastic terms, such as KoSoYoung (the name of a famous Korean actress), which stood for *Ko*rea University (Lee graduated), *So*mang Presbyterian Church (Lee attended) and the *Young*nam Province (Lee's hometown) (Moon, 2009). The inference here was that his cabinet candidates came from a small and specific pool based on certain regional, religious and university affiliation. To make the situation worse, most of his cabinet members faced a series of corruption charges and ministerial candidates nominated were involved in legislation violations. Furthermore, Lee himself was charged in multiple corruption cases and surrounded by rumours about his relationship with BBK and LTE Bank.

After his inauguration, the Lee government proposed a pressing agenda which included a revival of the national economy through deregulation, privatization, lower tax rates and further free trade agreements with major economic partners. Lee's foreign policy aimed at abandoning the Sunshine Policy and restoring an alliance with the US. However, as much as Lee wanted to be CEO of 'Korea Inc.,' his leadership disregarded the democratic process of consensus-building across political parties and the general public interest. For example, Lee announced that his government was going to lift the ban on imports of American beef after a meeting with President Bush. The ban was used as a precautionary measure after mad cow disease broke out in the United States. His announcement triggered mass protests. The Lee government reacted quickly and deployed the police to suppress the protests by force and blamed radicals and pro-North Korean leftists for the unrest. However, the protests continued to grow. More than one million people protested in the heart of Seoul, calling for renegotiation with the United States and Lee's resignation. The protest ended with Lee's official apology, the replacement of presidential aides and renegotiation (Moon, 2009). Following Lee's leadership as CEO of Korea Inc., he proposed an ambitious project named 'Pan-Korea Grand Waterway'. The project involved a 540km-long canal construction which connected Seoul and Busan and then extended to four major rivers running through the country. Immense benefits were to be derived nationwide by greatly improving water quality, serving as an important infrastructure for tourism and transportation for commercial goods, and for the prevention of natural disasters. As with his announcement of imports of American beef, his proposal was resisted by opposition parties and civil society groups because of environmental and economic concerns. The project was later renamed 'Four Major Rivers Restoration Project' and became a five-year plan to maintain water resources for drought and flooding, to improve water quality and restore ecosystems. However, the legitimacy of the project was questioned by the public. This USD 33 billion construction project had minimal impact in creating jobs and generated approximately USD 200 million of illegal cash flow to major construction companies.

With regard to Lee's foreign policy, it further polarized politics in Korea. Lee remained highly sceptical of the Sunshine Policy and planned to restore a security alliance with the United States. His foreign policy was welcomed by Washington. At the G20 meeting in 2010, the alliance was described as the linchpin of security for Korea and the United States as well as for the Pacific as a whole (Glosserman and Santoro, 2012). In return, Lee supported all Washington policies, ranging from climate change, non-proliferation of weapons of mass destruction and free trade agreements. Although relations with the United States was restored at the cost of public interest, the Lee government's foreign policy deteriorated inter-Korean relations further. Controversy flared up when a Korean tourist was killed during her tour of the Hundai-run Mount Geumgang. This event was followed by the Cheonan warship sinking incident, which escalated tensions. Korea launched an investigation by experts from five countries and concluded that the incident was the result of a North Korean torpedo attack. However, according to Russia's and China's investigation, there was no definite evidence to confirm that North Korea had carried out the attack. In addition to the ambiguity, the timing of releasing investigation results was dubious since the results were announced on the very day the fifth local election campaign commenced. Lee and his government were heavily criticized for using the incident to manipulate the election.

To sum up, Lee Myung-bak's political rise was possible due to his successful mobilization of Korea's yearning for an economic miracle. However, the reality was a further deterioration of the national economy during Lee's presidency. Even considering the global financial crisis, the average growth during the Lee government was 2.92 per cent which was 2 per cent lower than the average in member states of the Organization for Economic Cooperation and Development (OECD, 2017) during the same period. His CEO-style leadership downgraded the quality of democracy in Korea. Moreover, his pro-US policy backfired and caused China's uneasy feelings toward Seoul.

With regard to economic policy, the sweeping and sudden departure from the previous regimes' (Kim and Roh) state-mobilized overseas direct investment may be seen as a retreat of the state from economic management. This process of reform represents a 'hybrid of pell-mell economic globalization' (Dittmer, 2002: 22) process in Korea, whereby the state is highly selective in embracing the principal values of globalization as well as in adopting its values for economic and industrial development. At the same time, the state resists transformation either of its role as a normative regime (the state as rational and unitary) or as representative of the political and economic culture (developmentalism and economic nationalism) (Dittmer, 2002). As Samuel S. Kim notes, 'For a trading state like Korea, with an extremely high trade/GNP product ratio, the extent of its openness and transparency and the degree of its global competitiveness correlate most closely with globalization in only one domain: economic globalization' (2000: 8).

Lowell Dittmer's (2002) and Samuel S. Kim's (2000) descriptions of the hybrid nature of Korean economic globalization can also be seen in the Lee Myung-bak administration's (2008–2013) newly adopted national development paradigm. Announced in 2009 as the 'low-carbon green growth' or *Jeotanso Noksaeksungjang* strategy, it included four major river restorations, green transportation (e.g. green cars), waste resource catchment and recycling projects (Choi, 2011). As in previous regimes, Lee Myung-bak's new governing ideology was a result of the state's conscious strategic response to the external stimuli linked to the global financial crisis in 2008, global emission reduction requirements under the post-Kyoto systems and ever-increasing competition with China (Choi, 2011). Aimed at creating greater employment and GDP growth driven by emissions reductions, the Lee Myung-bak regime's growth strategy was no different from the strategy of previous economic nationalist regimes.

Under Lee Myung-bak, the state maintained a strategic role in regulating domestic and international market forces, and in coordinating industrial changes with strong administrative guidance through the Ministry of Knowledge and Economy, thus harnessing these driving forces for the national economic interest. As was the case with Korea's inward FDI-led economic globalization strategy, the green-growth strategy should be considered primarily within the political economy spectrum, in which the state is a rational and unitary actor. The various plans of the Kim Dae-jung (1998–2003), Roh Moo-hyun (2003–2008) and Lee Myung-bak (2008–2013) regimes to embrace neoliberal globalization principles, including active encouragement of inward FDI, have not reversed the traditional nationalist development trajectory. Rather, the process has strengthened the state's capacity. The adoption of neoliberal economic activities, such as lifting certain trade barriers and encouraging foreign direct investment, was necessary to assist certain areas of the economy to overcome a currency crisis and was therefore judged to be in the national interest. However, these economic activities were subordinate to the goal of state building and the interests of the state. Hence, 'deepening globalization has become a state mantra for moving beyond crisis' and developmentalist state models to 'a modernized, globalized, market-driven and mass-consumption economy' (Hall, 2004: 84).

The Park Geun-hye presidency

Park Geun-hye won the presidential election in 2012. She was born in 1952 as the eldest daughter of Park Chung-hee who was the most admired national leader in numerous public opinion polls. She began her political career as the *de facto* first lady after her mother was assassinated in 1974. Until 1998, she remained completely 'invisible' and resumed her political career in a supplementary election. After her resumption, she quickly emerged as an iconic figure for conservatives and gained extensive support among voters. First, she sought to define a separate political brand for herself and thus distanced herself from the Lee Myung-bak administration. This was particularly evident in the Sejong city controversy. The administration had tried to reverse the reform implemented by the previous Roh administration, relocating state departments from Seoul to Sejong city. Park opposed Lee's attempt, in effect playing the role of opposition within the conservative party. Second, Korean society remained male-dominated with women occupying marginal socioeconomic and political positions. A 'prepared female president' was among the slogans put forward by the Park campaign, emphasizing how meaningful it would be – not just for Korea, but East Asia as a whole – to have a first female president. Third, Park competed aggressively with the progressives over the issues of economic democratization and welfare reform (Kim, 2014).

Being a conservative leader, Park had championed neo-liberal policy agendas. Some of her campaign promises included a gradual returning of the Wartime Operational Control by 2015, awarding about USD 180 monthly to support senior citizens (65 years old and older), having government pay the entire medical expenses for four major diseases, embracing economic democratization and fairness in the market, starting a trust-building process with North Korea, and cutting taxes. It was believed by the public that she would be trustworthy given the memory of her mother as a caring figure and her father as a strong leader.

After her presidential inauguration, Park placed great emphasis on complying with what she had promised to the people during her campaign and placed great weight on trust between the people and government. Based on this desire to win the trust of the people, the Park administration proclaimed as one of its aims the happiness of the people and a new era of hope. To be specific, the Park administration intended to bring about a creative economy with an emphasis on jobs, tailored employment and welfare, ingenious education and culture, social safety and integration, and the establishment of the foundations of a unification era directed toward the attainment of happiness. Park intended to open a new hopeful era where every citizen in Korea could feel happy based on the trust of the people, 'Trust net' was the intangible but essential infrastructure without which Korea could enter into the club of most advanced countries.

Trust was not just confined to domestic politics; it was a government philosophy, often called 'trustpolitik', encompassing both international relations and inter-Korean relations. Counting on strong defence, the Park government was fully prepared to deal with any kind of North Korean provocation and was determined to let North Korea pay an appropriate price for such an act. As Park repeatedly clarified, Korea would not accept North Korea as a nuclear weapon state and would make every effort to negotiate an end to its nuclear capabilities. While North Korean nuclear weapons and threats remained, Seoul would reinforce its own defence capabilities and adjust its nuclear deterrence posture with the United States to meet pending nuclear threats from North Korea. Parks also underlined the importance of trust in international relations. She quoted a Chinese aphorism 'nothing is possible without trust', hoping to improve relations with China based on mutual trust.

In terms of her economic policy, Park put forward a vision for creating a 'Second Miracle on the Han River' through the development of a 'creative economy'. Park and her administration introduced its 'Creative Economy Action Plan' and launched a new Ministry of Science, Information and Communications Technologies, and Future Planning to lead in developing, coordinating and implementing related policies. The administration eased regulations, developed the underperforming services sectors and eliminated bureaucratic silos. She encouraged start-up firms and held highly-publicized meetings with internationally famous entrepreneurs, including Microsoft founder Bill Gates and Google co-founder and CEO Larry Page. This agenda presented new opportunities for cooperation with the US (Connell, 2013). With extensive trade and investment interconnections, the two countries would benefit from collaboration and share best practices for fostering innovation and entrepreneurship. However, this agenda was a long-term process extending beyond Park's five-year term; success depended on consistency and public perceptions towards creativity.

After four years in office, President Park was impeached by the National Assembly for violations of the constitution and the law, including extortion and abuse of power, leaking confidential government documents and information to her long-time friend, and soliciting bribes from the *Chaebol*. The verdict was confirmed in 2017. The events which led to Park's impeachment revealed how much democracy in Korea had undermined and how thoroughly the country's leader had privatized political power mandated by the people. Moreover, the impeachment itself demonstrated how much democracy has matured.

The Moon Jae-in presidency

Moon Jae-in came into office in May 2017 following the influence-peddling scandal of the Park administration. Moon had been appointed senior secretary for civil affairs in Roh's presidential administration (2003–2008). Throughout Roh's presidency, Moon's prominent role earned him the nickname 'Shadow of Roh'. Although he was one of Roh's most trusted advisors, he largely sought to avoid the public attention that typically accompanies such a position. In 2004, Roh was the target of an impeachment attempt by the opposition, and Moon joined the legal team that argued Roh's case before the constitutional court. Later that year, he oversaw the opening of the Kaesong Industrial Complex in North Korea. The Kaesong venture was one of the most famous expressions of the Roh administration's attempt to engage with North Korea. It represented a continuation of the Sunshine Policy initiated by Roh's predecessor, President Kim Dae-jung as discussed above. In 2007, being chief of staff in Roh's administration, Moon was the principal organizer of a historic summit between Roh and the North Korean leader Kim Jong-il in October 2007. That meeting led to an ambitious eight-point plan designed to bring peace to the Korean peninsula.

Moon entered electoral politics for the first time in 2012. In 2016 Park's impeachment triggered a snap election. Moon quickly emerged as the front runner. During his campaign, Moon pledged to rein in the power of the *Chaebol*, to sever the ties between government and business, and to adopt a more sensible North Korea Policy.

Since his inauguration, he attempted to portray himself as an accessible president, opening his office's website as a platform for the public to lodge petitions and making it mandatory for the Blue House to respond if 200,000 signatures were gathered within 30 days. After one year in office Moon's approval rating hovered around mid-80 per cent and was the highest achieved by any president after just one year in office. However, it was questioned whether much of this popularity was based on Moon's charisma.

With regard to Moon's economic policies, his administration recognized that average Korean households had accumulated very high levels of debt, while at the same time incomes had stagnated in the previous three years. Korea's debt structure at the time encompassed many interdependencies, thus an inability in one subsection of society to repay its debt had the potential to spark serious repercussions across the entire Korean financial system. Consequently, it was important that Koreans are given the ability to pay off their debts. Within such context, a supplementary budget was passed in June 2017, adding funds for the creation of about 63,000 public sector jobs. The original budget proposal called for the creation of 71,000 but this figure was reduced after negotiations in the National Assembly as Moon's party only held 39 per cent of seats. This budget was the first step in meeting Moon's campaign promise of creating 810,000 public sector jobs by the end of his term. Following this budget proposal, a budget proposal for 2018 fiscal year was submitted, which set a target of creating 174,000 more public sector jobs by 2022. In this proposal, an increase of 16 per cent of the minimum wage from year to year was approved. Given the high popularity of the minimum wage policy during the presidential election, the 2017 increase was not contested by lawmakers and led to the subsequent annual increases desired by the Moon administration. An important and unexpected development accompanying the minimum wage increase has been the advent of compulsory holidays implemented by employers. These holidays have become a common device to ensure that the pay of employees paid through an annual salary system conforms to the new minimum wage. Instead of raising salaries to meet the new standards, several companies and organizations such as universities have instituted compulsory holidays to reduce the number of workdays. Many workers have complained that this makes their jobs harder because the amount of the actual work they need to do remains unchanged despite now having less time. Given this early stage of Moon's economic policies, it is hard to tell whether wage increases are hurting the economy in any significant way.

As for inter-Korean relations, Moon advocated for a firm but patient strategy in engaging with North Korea. He expressed his willingness to go to Pyongyang under the right circumstances and to establish peace on the Korean Peninsula. His enthusiasm for a more activist approach toward the inter-Korean relations contrasted with the freeze in inter-Korean relations that had developed during the more conservative reciprocity-based strategy favoured by his predecessors Presidents Park and Lee.

In his Berlin Declaration, Moon sent a message to Pyongyang that the new government in Seoul was willing to reset the course of inter-Korean relations, which had turned very hostile during the last decade. The Moon government's choice of Berlin as the location in which to declare his Korean Peninsula Peace Initiative is symbolic. German Unification has always been a motivation for Korean politicians in approaching the question of unification on the Korean Peninsula and has drawn lessons from the German experience. Moon thus defined unification as a process rather than an end, which demands continuity and consistency in the policies of engagement and cooperation despite domestic political change. The Korean Peninsula Peace Initiative outlines five policy directions and broad objectives including the overall thrust on achieving peace in the Korean Peninsula as the primary goal, denuclearization of the Korean Peninsula, institutionalization of the peace process in inter-Korean relations, direct inter-Korean economic cooperation and separation of non-political exchange between the two Koreas from military and political issues. Moon's Berlin Doctrine was a substantive proposal. However, the prospect of bringing back inter-Korean relations to that of the Sunshine era is limited (John, 2017).

The third inter-Korean summit between President Moon Jae-in and Chairman Kim Jong-un was held in Pyongyang, capitol of North Korea between 18 and 20 September 2018, although the two Koreas initially had different views about the date and agenda of the summit. Given the diversity and complexity of the Korean Peninsula issues, no conclusion can be drawn until various options are secured. At this stage, Moon is aware of the criticisms that Korean conservatives have raised against the Sunshine Policy proposed by the Kim government. The Moon government has refrained from offering Pyongyang any concessions prior to the upcoming inter-Korean summit. Economic aid has been kept to a minimum, even though Moon ran on a platform calling for its resumption. Meanwhile, the Moon government has gone out of its way to court President Trump and praise his maximum pressure policy as key to North Korea's call for summits with the United States and Korea.

To sum up, the Korean political system under democracy has become much more complex and difficult with numerous political stakeholders and a diverse and active civil society. In order to achieve the completion of democratic consolidation, political leaders need to be equipped with the democratic leadership skills of political compromise, and civil society is required to accept the rule of law and partake responsibly in the political process. However, under the existing constitution, the Korean political system is inherently unstable as a result of the instability and factionalism of its political parties and the single five-year term of the presidency. Korean political parties, built around the leaders' personality and regionalism, are poorly institutionalized. They are unable to develop stable party politics and are vulnerable to corruption. Under the single five-year term, presidential candidates are likely to make impractical policy promises, and once elected, the president has strong incentives to pursue short-run economic programs. Once disenchanted with the president, electorates are likely to elect opposition party members to the National Assembly and resort to mass civic protests, raising the prospect of minority government and political deadlock. Under such political instability, the government is less likely to meet the success policy criteria with institutional reforms and economic policy measures. Concurrently, society has become aware of the lack of decisiveness, consistency, credibility and long-term orientation of development policies, which renders the task of reaching policy consensus more difficult.

Government-business relations

The major determinants of Korea's phenomenal economic success have been the subject of debate among economists, political scientists and political economists, and institutionalists. Literature advances a range of explanations, from market mechanisms to the strong role of the state and the role of state policy in facilitating private and public sector coordination.

Considerable debate about Korea's developmental capitalism over three decades (1960s-1980s) occurred among neo-liberal economists who attribute the country's rapid economic growth to the pursuit of export-oriented industrialization (EOI) along with policies that favour a market orientation and minimal state intervention (Krueger, 1982, 1990; Little, 1990; Riedel, 1988; Westphal, 1978, 1990). Political economists have focused on domestic political processes and structures in Korea (Amsden, 1987a, 1987b, 1992, 1994; Chu, 1989; Haggard and Moon, 1990; Haggard, 2000; Kuznets, 1985; Moon, 1988; Wade, 1988a, 1988b, 1992; White and Wade, 1988; Weiss, 1998, Woo, 1991; Woo-Cumings, 2003). In spite of this considerable debate, the general consensus has been that the Korean state has intervened in the market as the *primum mobile* of socioeconomic and cultural progress. In other words, Korea's economic success and its place at the top of the economic hierarchy among developing countries is a product not of culture, geography or uninhibited market forces, but of the actions and institutions of a developmental state (Hart-Landsberg, Jeong and Westra, 2007). Robert Gilpin's neo-realist approach (neo-mercantilism to economic nationalism) captures well the Korean case in which 'economic activities are and should be subordinate to the goal of state-building and the interests of the state' (quoted in Crane, 1998: 57).

Liberal market economists or neo-classical theorists have pointed out Korea's high-speed economic growth in its pursuit of EOI along with policies that favour a market orientation and minimal government intervention (Westphal, 1978, 1990; Krueger, 1982, 1990; Riedel, 1988; Little, 1990). These writers also emphasize that the success of Korea's industrialization was mainly due to the fact that Korea adopted a 'neutral policy' regime in which free trade and private markets played a major role. According to the aforementioned theorists, government intervention in economic markets creates distortion and breeds inefficiency; instead, the free play of market forces should be promoted. For example, Krueger argues against the restrictive 'direct control' of ISI regimes, which she maintains, 'fight the market' and lead to a highly complex and erratic incentive structure which eventually results in a decline in output and productivity. Krueger links Korea's rapid growth rather to their reliance on EOI.

While the neo-classical approach attempts to explain the rise of the Korean economy in terms of the shifting patterns of comparative advantage and its management, a new breed of scholars, known as statists, have begun to study domestic political processes and structures in Korea in relation to its rapid economic growth. Despite the considerable debate about the character of successive post-war Korean governments, the consensus of the literature is perhaps most evident in its view of state dominance over economy, market and labour. What really matters in the context of Korea's economic success from the statist perspective, are the domestic political structures that shape policy choices and implementation, and ultimately determine economic outcomes (Jones and Sakong, 1980; Moon, 1988; Wade, 1988; Woo, 1991). Statists suggest that rather than emphasizing policy itself, the nature of economic policy-making should first be analyzed in examining the nature of Korean economic development. Accordingly, the adoption of an EOI strategy is not a result of market forces, but of a conscious state choice to realize economic and political objectives. The state's consistent and coherent implementation has been facilitated by the state's strength unique to Korea. In particular, Amsden's work on Korean industrialization challenges the free-market orthodoxy (Amsden, 1987a, 1987b, 1992, 1994). The crux of Amsden's argument is that although low wages and the exclusion of the popular sector are the foundation of Korea's successful late industrialization, low wages themselves are not adequate stimuli for success, nor does the pursuit of comparative advantage ensure success. Instead, pervasive state intervention, combined with large-scale guaranteed external sources including technological and foreign capital (i.e. aid and loans),[5] is effective and necessary to produce a nation's dynamic comparative advantage. In short, the state interventionist nature of the Korean political economy is probably the most critical aspect of Korea's first phase of EOI industrialization.

The Korean experience of economic development is unique in the world. Before the Japanese occupation of Korea, China had been the prevailing influence in Korea, and Korea's tradition of centralized and bureaucratic government is often considered the principal example of this influence. During the Japanese occupation (1910–1945), more companies were established with large landowners becoming the most influential entrepreneurs. From 1946–1961, Korea depended heavily upon other countries, mainly the United States, for aid and capital. This made Korea one of the highest aid-receiving countries in the world. During the 1960s to 1970s, the Korean government was in pursuit of industrialization of the economy. The developmental state was the dominant economic ideology in Korea. The government targeted particular industries for support, which led to close government-business relations. '[T]he government and the private sector ... developed a "big-push partnership' in which the government shared the investment risks of the private sector and provided support largely based on performance in competitive markets ... export-oriented industrialization and human resource development, as encapsulated in the slogans "exportation of all industries" and "scientification of all people", capture the essence of Korea's approach' (Kim, 2011: 13–14). With export-oriented industrialization, the 'infant industry' was protected by government until the firms became competitive in the work marketplace. However, such close government-business ties carried risks.

The close government-business relationship, characterized as 'Korea Inc.,' constituted an environment where corruption could thrive because of the lack of institutional oversight (Chamberlin, 2001). In the Korean context, this meant that bank owners were not required to account for the bad loans that they made to the *Chaebol* because they knew the government would bail them out in any case. Banks typically lent money to businesses without regard for the viability or transparency of the loans.

In the 1990s, with democratic transition and consolidation, the private sector, especially the *Chaebol*, became more assertive in lobbying against unwanted controls by the government and openly supporting sympathetic candidates. As the Hanbo Steel collapse of 1997 indicated, democracy provided new channels for business influence through the National Assembly. In this sense, President Kim Dae-Jung was put under continual political pressure from labour, students, civic organizations and the public-to 'do something' about the increasing concentration of business and corporate malfeasance and corruption. Political battles were waged over the nature of business-government relations which, in turn, became the main policy agenda for the Kim Dae-Jung administration (Haggard, 1999).

On the eve of the 1997–1998 financial crisis, the necessity for structural reform of the Korean economy was widely known and debated. Korea's development strategies in the preceding decades had been characterized by preoccupation with economic growth and less concern with social development, concentration of economic power around large business groups, which generally weakened the position of small and medium-sized business firms, and immature or undeveloped industrial relations that led to militancy in labour-management disputes (Judd and Lee, 2000). These characteristics would lead to more serious structural problems in the Korean economy that required rectification and reform. Since then (late 1997), the leading *Chaebol* faced major financial challenges, followed by a broadly-based government campaign to severely diminish their power and reach.

In 1998, President Kim Dae-jung initiated substantial *anti-Chaebol* policies aimed at all major controversial elements of *Chaebol* corporate governance. It proceeded through a dense legislation-backed institutional framework, but one that left the *Chaebol* space to negotiate, delay or resist. Given the depths of the *Chaebol*'s crisis, they agreed to a 'five-principle' restructuring plan for corporate governance and the establishment of a Financial Supervisory Commission for the implementation of the plan (Kim, Hoskisson, Tihanyi and Hong 2004). The government also strongly encouraged minority shareholder activism through legislation. It strengthened shareholder rights through revisions to commercial codes and security exchange laws, and removed restrictions on institutional investors. To empower minority shareholders seeking greater managerial transparency and accountability, the government also legislated substantially reduced shareholding thresholds necessary for initiating action. The threshold for filing a derivative lawsuit against management was dropped from 1 to 0.01 per cent of outstanding shares. The threshold for inspecting the financial records of listed companies was lowered from 3 to 1 per cent. The introduction of proxy voting also appeared to offer minority shareholders the opportunity to elect directors to represent their own interests. The government also introduced a mandatory outside director scheme. Companies with assets of over 2 trillion won had to have over half their board seats allocated to outside directors (Jang and Kim, 2002). However, these policies had limited impact on the *Chaebol*. During the Roh presidency, the *Chaebol* had regained some of their lost standing due to their ability to earn the foreign currency that was needed to repay foreign debt and recover from the financial crisis. Suddenly the *Chaebol* were again the saviours of the national economy (Kalinowski, 2009). In 2007, the election of President Lee marked the end of temporary corporatism and state autonomy. The Lee administration turned to *Chaebol*-friendly policies that focused government spending on supporting the *Chaebol* and continued market reforms that benefitted the conglomerates. Similarly to the Lee administration, Park Geun-hye proposed to separate the financial capital held by the large enterprises from their industrial capital by revising the Securities Exchange Act of the Republic of Korea to place a fundamental prohibition on cross shareholdings by large enterprises, in a bid to achieve 'economic democratization'. The Moon administration, on the other hand, aimed at reforming the *Chaebol* and set up equitable competitive order, in clear distinction to the Lee Myung-bak administration.

Conclusion

Today Korea is the eleventh largest economy in the world and can boast of high technology, a steady and relatively high growth rate, generally stable government, low criminal rates, healthy economic sectors, good prospects for further growth, and an exceptional level of human capital development (Sanidas, 2017). Korea's success story reflects the government's success in achieving fundamentals right, such as high rates of literacy, high savings and investment rates, and low inflation rates that stayed within the bounds of an outward-oriented economy (Clifford, 2016). After decades of attempts at democracy, Korea has experienced a full turnaround from two progressive governments (1998–2008) to two conservative ones (2008–2017). With the rise of the Moon government, it remains to be seen how the new president will perform and whether he will be able to run a clean government free of corruption scandals and bring reconciliation and national unity to the Korean society that is polarized in terms of wealth, ideology, region and generation.

Notes

1 The term *Chaebol*, which in Korean literally means a group of financial cliques, indicates mostly family-owned and managed conglomerates such as Samsung, LG, SK and Hyundai. They exist in a similar way to the pre-Second World War zaibatsu groups in Japan, highly centralized family (mostly) controlled financial and industrial business conglomerates during the imperial period of Japan. They exercise monopolistic and oligopolistic control across product lines and industries. *Chaebol* (Korean pronunciation of zaibatsu but same word in Chinese (i.e. 財閥)), are similar to the zaibatsu in that they are prestigious, powerful and influential, and their corporate behaviour largely determines the competitive climate. Korea is to a large extent a command economy and the mechanism by which economic commands are affected is the *Chaebol*. During the rapid growth period (1960s-1980s), the Korean state chose to favour the *Chaebol* for most of its business affairs as a means of accelerating the national priority to fast track economic growth. This tight collusion between state and business inevitably led to inequality between the *Chaebol* and small and medium-sized companies, between social classes, and between industrial sectors.
2 Korea has had a long history of economic nationalism stimulated initially by a negative response to earlier interactions with foreign regimes, and then by the desperate need for economic survival. This nationalistic economic doctrine has been the binding force that have given direction to Korea's industrialization policies over the last half-century (Lopez-Aymes 2010). Furthermore, a strong belief in self-sufficiency has inevitably resulted in a tough business climate, seemingly especially hostile to foreign companies.
3 One of the most striking features of the global political economic geography in the twenty-first century is the shift in countries' traditional policy orientation based on market-driven multilateralism. Among the most noticeable features of the new global development is the stepping up of economic regionalism efforts towards integration and cooperation (regional trade agreement/free trade agreement) particularly in Asia. As of June 2017, 659 Regional Trade Agreement (RTAs) notifications had been received by the General Agreement on Tariffs and Trade (GATT) then the World Trade Organisation (WTO). These WTO figures correspond to 445 physical RTAs of which 279 are currently in force. Over 20 per cent of the 279 RTAs were FTAs (free trade agreements) in which one of the signatories was an East Asian country (World Trade Organisation, 2017). With a growing interest in institutional economic integration, Korea has become one of the most active nations in Asia in the context of regional economic integration.
4 Chennggycheon is an 11km-long modern stream bisecting downtown Seoul (Capital of Korea). The restoration and renewal of the Cheggycheon into an open and modern recreation space in downtown Seoul started in July 2003 and was completed in September 2005.
5 The Korean War (1950–1953) provided the Rhee Syngman regime (1948–1960) with the legitimacy to expand the military and police, and led it to promote an active incorporation into the global capitalist economy, largely supported by foreign capital (American aid). This eventually enabled the Park Chung-hee regime (1963–1979) to dominate the economic and financial sectors (Choi, 1993: 22).

Part II

Korea's mature economy

Perceptions of Korea-based MNCs

3 Interviews with multinational corporations (MNCs) in Korea

Chapter 2 of this book reviewed the most striking features of the Korean economy in the late twentieth century (i.e. the rise to and fall from economic eminence). During the 1970s and 1980s Korea achieved the most spectacular economic growth among the developing countries. Yet, in the latter part of 1997 (Asian Financial Crisis), Korea became the first country to receive what was then a record-breaking rescue package from the International Monetary Fund (IMF) to remedy its ailing economy. It was obvious that Korea's state-led growth model, embedded in a developmental leadership approach, faced the challenges (i.e. IMF remedy packages for the Korean financial crisis[1]) presented by the unavoidable free, market-driven globalization forces and resulted in radical transformation of Korea's long-standing economic growth model (Rodier 2014). These challenges have led the Korean government to a dramatic shift towards a neo-liberal foreign direct investment (FDI) and free trade agreement (FTA)-oriented international trade model. The combination of institutional reforms in favour of sweeping liberalization measures and pro-foreign direct investment (FDI) enabled Korea to record a dramatic increase in inward FDI since the late1990s (Kim and Lee, 2007). This radical change was marked by a substantial opening of the domestic market to foreign capital and seemingly favourable attitudes towards foreign capital in the state's strategic policy direction under the banner of globalization, thus tracing Korea's new economic trajectory since the 2000s. This impressive and positive portrayal of Korea's openness to trade and FDI in the aftermath of the financial crisis should not however mislead readers by disguising the fact that Korea's reform measures have not proceeded smoothly, due to the painful and difficult decisions that had to be made along the road towards conforming to global standards.

With the arrival of Kim Dae-jung's administration and its vision of transforming the nation into a Northeast Asian business hub, and subsequently Roh Moo-hyun's new vision of Korea as Research and Development (R&D) centre for MNCs, Korea's industrial development paradigm has undergone a new and radical shift in the economic and business spheres, particularly towards a new market-oriented paradigm in place of the old model of the developmental state. In particular, the rapid rise of emerging markets (i.e. BRICS) in recent years and the aggressive push to invite foreign R&D centres to these emerging countries have put a brake on the rising number of foreign R&D centres in Korea. China has been making a meteoric rise as the focal point for global R&D centres on the back of its massive manpower and comprehensive government funding to support foreign R&D centres. As a result, Korea finds itself standing at a crossroads where it earnestly needs to establish and realize a new growth paradigm for R&D in close collaboration with multinational corporations (MNCs).

As will be shown in this chapter, the most striking finding from the qualitative data analysis of in-depth interviews substantiates the view that as Korea looks to the next decade and beyond, the country will continue to grapple with the challenges of improving its nation image in the face of increasing competition globally. While the interview results in this study are based on earlier fieldwork conducted in Korea in 2010 and 2015, these findings are still valid in 2018 given that the negative image of the Korean market is often regarded as one of the risk factors that make many MNCs choose other markets over Korea to this day (*The Business Times*, 2018). The data shows that the collective nature of economic nationalism (i.e. market access barriers in the form of regulations/rules against foreign businesses in Korea) mobilized by the state is still perceived by MNCs as prevalent in Korea despite the rapid development of globalization and cosmopolitanism.

Against this backdrop, this chapter offers data analysis on MNCs' perception of Korea's new economic trajectory (FDI-driven market economy) and Korea's capabilities to attract foreign R&D centres, as well as the factors driving MNC investment. The data was collected from the fieldwork performed in Korea comprising empirical evidence of the results from one-on-one interviews with MNCs operating in Korea. Specifically, an analysis of in-depth interviews with 49 executives was made with the aim of identifying factors that have affected decisions to establish R&D centres in Korea and to set future investment directions. The interviewees include the CEOs of foreign investment companies (R&D-driven) and the chairmen of foreign chambers of commerce in Korea. The interviews were conducted in 2010 and the years between 2011 and 2015.

Rather than limiting our analysis to a theoretical framework in order to highlight the real capabilities and limitations of Korea in attracting foreign R&D centres, in this chapter we use the case studies of two multinational companies (one from the US and one from Germany) which established their R&D centres in Korea and engaged in R&D activities. These two companies were chosen as case study subjects because their purpose of having established their R&D centres in Korea is different from that of other foreign investment companies, which aim to undertake research and development/engineering or supply parts/materials to Korean conglomerates such as Samsung, Hyundai and LG. In contrast, the two chosen companies established their Centres for Excellence, designed to play a pivotal role in realizing sustainable future growth. These companies have plans to continue establishing their key future Centres for Excellence on the back of continuous growth which they have witnessed for the last ten years. The plans carry important implications for Gyeonggi-do (Gyeonggi Province) in attracting more R&D FDI and implementing Korea's strategies to be the R&D hub in Northeast Asia, as well as increasing by extension the number of foreign R&D centres.

Chapter 2 of this book explored the process by which economic nationalism as an economic trajectory was challenged in Korea during the post-WWII era of globalization. The chapter argues that no economic trajectory shift has occurred in the course of Korea's neo-liberal economic trajectory initiated by the Kim Dae-jung administration in response to the 1997 financial crisis. The significant increase of foreign capital in Korea from the late 1990s has been closely related to the Korean state's change in economic policies, particularly towards foreign capital. These economic activities, whether neo-liberal or neo-mercantilist, adopted during the process of capitalist industrialization in this era of economic globalization, are still found to be subordinate to the goal of state building and the interests of the state. This observation suggests a very different consideration from the tradition of economic liberalism, which emphasizes factor endowments. In fact, the study reveals that the Korean regimes' 'liberal motivation for liberalization' has been directed and promoted by developmental and neo-mercantilist policies.

Economic globalization and economic nationalism in Korea as perceived by MNCs

Following its independence from the Japanese in 1945, it was inconceivable that Korea would become one of the world's most dynamic economies. However, the nation has recorded an annual average economic growth of 9 per cent over the last four decades and, despite suffering heavily under the 1997 financial crisis, Korea was the fifteenth largest economy in the world in 2011 based on nominal gross domestic product (GDP).

One notable characteristic found in the country's rapid economic growth and development was that its success would have been unlikely without strong economic nationalism (EN), stimulated initially by a negative response to earlier interactions with foreign regimes, and then by the desperate need for economic survival. This nationalistic economic doctrine has been the binding force that has given direction to Korea's modernization policies over the last half-century (Lopez-Aymes, 2010; Cho, 2008). Its growth mantra of development, productivity and competitiveness "constitutes the foremost and single-minded priority of state action", directing its (state) focus towards managing and protecting the domestic economy, labour and even capital flows (Baughn and Yaprak, 1996), with a strong focus on promoting domestic capitalists, and thus national interest (economic development) (Dent, 2000; Amsden, 1987a; Jones and Sakong, 1980; Wade, 1990; Woo, 1991; Onis, 1991). The state's authoritarian and corporatist structures that underpin the processes of capital accumulation, its state-allocated monopolies and a reliance on the international economy in the form of foreign capital (e.g. aid and loans) have been identified as the key forces that pushed Korea's growth trajectory in a highly nationalistic direction (Amsden, 1987b; Chu, 1989; Jones and Sakong, 1980; Wade, 1990; Woo, 1991).[2]

Ironically, successful economic growth and accumulated economic wealth have led to escalating wealth accumulation and increased consumption of foreign material goods, particularly western products (Schütte and Ciarlante, 1998). In comparison with the 1980s, when Korea first began to import a small number of products, such as cigarettes and cars, an ever-increasing level of buying power has given present-day Koreans access to a wider range of foreign products. Many of these products were not available in the Korean market a decade ago (Yi, 2002). If a nation's level of globalization is to be measured by its economic openness to the global economy, that is, its consumption level of international media and foreign products, the movement of its capital, trade, investments and people across borders and the degree of extension into global markets,[3] then Korea certainly demonstrates this phenomenon.

Korea's 1997 financial crisis brought various serious economic problems to Korea. The GDP growth rate in the first quarter of 1998 was recorded at negative 3.8 per cent compared with the same quarter in 1997, which was the lowest since the negative 7.8 per cent growth rate recorded in 1980. Changes in unemployment and inflation rates were also remarkable. The unemployment rate rose drastically from 2.6 per cent at the end of November 1997, to 6.8 per cent by the end of 1998, and the number of unemployed exceeded 1.5 million (Moon, Lee and Yoo, 1999: 14). The consumer price index rose from 4.3 per cent in November 1997 to 7.5 per cent in 1998, largely due to the exchange rate devaluation (Moon, Lee and Yoo, 1999: 33). The most significant rise in unemployment was recorded in the manufacturing industry, particularly in sectors related to infrastructure and automobiles. The number of Korean companies bankrupted during the period January to April 1998 totalled 11,908, over 20 per cent of which were in export-related industries. Excluding gold exports, Korea's export growth rate was only 1.4 per cent in January 1998 and a negative growth rate was recorded in May 1998. Most significantly, overall trade surplus recorded a 35.9 per cent decrease in imports. Inevitably, despite its state-led export-driven growth model, embedded in a strong nationalistic and mercantilist leadership structure, Korea was forced to accept the neoliberal conditions of globalization (market democratization and minimization of state involvement) imposed by the International Monetary Fund (IMF) as a condition of its bailout of USD 58 billion in 1997.

As was found in previous regimes, the new government of Kim Dae-jung (1998–2002) began its term with the national goal of economic and industrial development. However, this time the government focused on attracting inward FDI (IFDI), with the initial aim of overcoming the currency crisis, followed by a strengthening of the competitiveness of Korean exports industry. This new economic strategy appeared contradictory to that of the previous decades of export-led industrialization, given that the role of IFDI throughout Korea's economic development had thus far been minimal and the government preferred to draw foreign loans as an alternative to encouraging IFDI.[4] In July 2002, Korea officially unveiled a detailed plan to transform the nation into a Northeast Asian hub. This new vision aimed to radically improve the market environment by expanding its focus on foreign investment, finance, logistics, information technology, manufacturing and research and development (R&D), and this became one of the Roh Moo-hyun administration's (2003–2008) ten national agendas.

The Roh regime established a special task force to develop and implement this new vision, specializing in the three specific sectors of logistics, finance and industry. The logistics dimension was considered to be crucial, given Korea's strategic business location between Japan and China. The Roh administration also pledged to improve the business and operating environment for MNCs through socio-economic and institutional reforms, such as labour market regulation, restructuring the *Chaebol*, liberalization of immigration policy and tax benefits for MNCs at the national level. As such, attracting MNCs became one of Korea's top economic priorities and formed the backbone of the globalization strategies adopted by the Kim and Roh administrations.

In the 1970s and even the early 1980s, the purchase and consumption of foreign consumer products (e.g. whiskies, cosmetics, food products and tobacco) were completely prohibited and were available only on the black market. However, today almost any foreign consumer product is obtainable in Korea from most small to medium and big department stores, as well as small shops. Even the tobacco industry, which has been the toughest industry to enter, shows strong growth compared to previous decades. Yet, many Koreans still tend to believe that their government was forced to adopt liberalization measures under external pressure during the 1997 financial crisis, rather than view these measures as being truly beneficial to themselves and to their own economy.

A survey of changes to Korea's international business environment from a foreign perspective, such as perceptions of the large corporations Samsung, Hyundai, LG and SK, Korean workers, management systems and improvements in living conditions after the 1997 financial crisis, has shown that there has been little evidence of improvement despite government efforts (Kwon, 2006). In order to verify this perception, face-to-face in-depth interviews were conducted in Korea between April and September 2010 with chief executive officers (CEOs) of foreign MNCs and four foreign chambers of commerce operating in Korea.

This book excludes postal and quantitative survey methods. Although a vast volume of samples can be secured with the quantitative survey method, there are many variables in the credibility of response, depending on the survey respondents' backgrounds and situations. Comprehensive and semi-structured in-depth interviews were chosen for this study, since the key to this study is the response level; in other words, how closely is the research topic (FDI in Korea and establishment of Research and Development Centre in Korea) related to the respondents and how accessible are the research subjects. The interviewees studied are CEOs or R&D division heads of global foreign investment companies which have already established or have plans to establish R&D centres in Korea. The interviews were conducted in advance via email or telephone. Among the interviewees, there were several chairmen of foreign chambers of commerce in Korea, including of the US, the UK, the EU and Australia. A total of 49 in-depth interviews were held; 12 companies between 11 and 16 April 2010; 28 companies between 28 June and 9 July; and 9 companies between 1 and 10 September, including four foreign chambers of commerce in Korea shown in Table 3.1. Listed by country, ten companies were from the US, ten from Germany, nine from Japan, four from the UK, two from Switzerland, two from France, one from Sweden, three from Australia, one from Taiwan and one company was Korean. In addition, a few foreign chambers of commerce were included; 22 foreign

Table 3.1 Interviewed companies

	Company name/ Nationality	Business area	Location
1	Envitec/Germany	Biogas	Gyeonggi province
2	Takada/Japan	Automotive	Gyeonggi province
3	GlaxoSmithKline/UK	Pharmaceutical	Seoul
4	Macquarie Bank/Australia	Banking	Seoul
5	Kim & Chang/Korea	Law firm	Seoul
6	European Chamber of Commerce	Chamber of commerce	Seoul
7	DHL/USA	Shipping	Seoul
8	UT-Innovation/USA	Innovation support	Gyeonggi province
9	3M/USA	Communication, medicine, stationery	Gyeonggi province
10	Merck/Germany	LED production	Gyeonggi province
11	Kimberly-Clark/USA	Health/hygiene goods	Gyeonggi province
12	Siemens Healthcare/ Germany	Radiology/experimental diagnosis	Gyeonggi province
13	Ericsson/Sweden	Telecommunication	Seoul
14	Rolls-Royce Marine/UK	Machinery, ship-building, automotive	Seoul
15	Envitec/Germany	Biogas	Gyeonggi province
16	NCK/Japan	Semi-conductor, LCD materials	Gyeonggi province
17	Renault-Samsung/France	Automotive	Seoul
18	Siemens Healthcare/ Germany	Radiology/experimental diagnosis	Gyeonggi province
19	GE Capital/USA	Banking, media	Seoul
20	Stemedica/USA	Stem cell	Gyeonggi province
21	Pax/USA	Consulting	Gyeonggi province
22	Kimberly-Clark/USA	Health/hygiene goods	Gyeonggi province
23	Robert Bosch/Germany	Automotive parts	Gyeonggi province
24	Bayer/Germany	Healthcare, advanced materials	Seoul
25	Kim & Chang/Korea	Law firm	Seoul
26	Novartis/Switzerland	Pharmaceutical/medicine	Seoul

	Company name/ Nationality	Business area	Location
27	Schneider Electric/France	Energy	Seoul
28	Delphi/ USA	Automotive parts	Gyeonggi province
29	Jatco/Japan	IT/Information security	Seoul
30	Dyesol-Timo/ Australia	Energy	Gyeonggi province
31	US Chamber of Commerce in Korea	Chamber of Commerce	Seoul
32	Hoya/Japan	Lens	Gyeonggi province
33	Jenoptik/Germany	Material processing laser System	Gyeonggi province
34	YC Optical/Japan	LCD display film	Gyeonggi province
35	SY Ink/Japan	Ink, Paint	Gyeonggi province
36	UK Chamber of Commerce	Chamber of Commerce	Seoul
37	Austrade	Trade representative	Seoul
38	Daihen/Japan	LCD Production equipment	Gyeonggi province
39	AvanStrate/Japan	Semi-conductor/Optics	Gyeonggi province
40	Mitsui-Kinzoku/Japan	Electric/electronics	Gyeonggi province
41	SC Bank/UK	Banking	Seoul
42	Ericsson/Sweden	Telecommunication	Seoul
43	Vector/Germany	IT	Seoul
44	Evonik Degussa/Germany	Fine Chemical	Seoul
45	Osram Korea/Germany	Lighting	Gyeonggi province
46	Hyatt/USA	Hotel	Seoul
47	Torayamk/Japan	Advanced materials	Seoul
48	FCI/Taiwan	Venture	Gyeonggi province
49	Berna Biotech/Switzerland	Pharmaceutical	Incheon

investment companies were based in Korea, ten of which had already established R&D centres or technical centres. The interviewees were chosen from very diverse industries, including automotive, IT, pharmaceutical, advanced materials, energy, radiology, semi-conductors, telemedicine, ship-building, LED/LCD and material processing laser systems, all of which are at the heart of the new growth paradigm for Korea as the R&D hub in Northeast Asia set on building its national competitiveness by attracting global R&D. Most of the interviews were held one-on-one or in groups (two or three interviewers for each interviewee) and took about 45–55 minutes on average. When interviewing the Japanese companies, an interpreter was in attendance. All the interviews were recorded and followed a semi-structured format. Given the highly sensitive nature of the data collected, confidentiality was assured, and the views of individual firms have not been provided in this Chapter.

Interviews were recorded, transcribed and subsequently interrogated, then deconstructed. Nvivo qualitative software was used for data analysis to identify the patterns, themes and causal-effects and relationships. This entailed categorizing respondents' comments according to their subject matter. The program then allowed all related comments and particular themes, to be viewed together. These comments were cross-referenced with the interview context so that, for example, it would be apparent whether the speakers were from Western or Asian firms, in which industry they were involved and so forth. Interviewees were invited to give their comments on the following questions:

- Clear background and reasons for choosing Korea to establish R&D centres (main functions of the R&D centres)
- Suitability of Korea for the establishment of a R&D centre
- Comments on Korea's strategies to attract R&D centres
- Comments on the future steps Korea needs to take in this regard
- The role of the *Chaebol* and the Korean government in the country's political economy and the impact on their businesses
- MNCs' understanding of the concept of globalization as viewed by the government and Korean companies (*Chaebol*) in general
- MNCs' perception of the feasibility of Korea becoming a R&D hub in Northeast Asia

Results of analysis

Is it realistic for Korea to aspire to become an R&D hub in Northeast Asia?

'The main purpose of foreign R&D centres is to develop advanced original technologies and these foreign R&D centres will bring with them a vast amount of technology,' said Mr. Jin Dae-je, then the founding minister of telecommunications (*The Dong-a Ilbo*, 29 May 2007). As has been mentioned earlier, the purpose of this study was to assess Korea's capabilities in attracting foreign R&D centres. The concept of a R&D centre, as has been referenced in the quote by Minister Jin, is seen to be based on the quantitative expansionist strategies pursued by the Korean government so far. In fact, since the 1997 Asian financial crisis, the number of R&D centres established by foreign investment companies with an investment of over USD 100,000 has jumped from less than 100 to 600, thanks to various investment promotion policies embedded in the foreign investment and technology transfer promotion laws. Although such quantitative expansion is significant, a clear understanding is necessary of how an increased number of foreign R&D centres contribute to the national economy. In October 2006, a survey of 105 foreign R&D centres in Korea was conducted by Korea Trade-Investment Promotion Agency (KOTRA) and Gallup Korea. According to the survey results, only 14 per cent of the centres had experienced a transfer of know-how in the past (*The Dong-a Ilbo*, 29 May 2007). Furthermore, Korea Industrial Technology Association indicated that as of 2007, only 7.4 per cent of foreign investment companies in Korea had established R&D centres in Korea. In other words, the Korean government's foreign investment promotion policies had yielded a result in the employment of highly skilled workers but not in the development of original technology or the transfer of know-how hoped for by the government when it invited foreign R&D centres. In fact, the interviewed foreign companies were found to have made little investment in the development of original technologies or the transfer of know-how. Bosch, a world-renowned German automotive parts manufacturer, Jenoptik, a laser materials processing company, Merck, a global top LCD seller, recently established their R&D centres in Korea specifically for purposes of research and development, as has been shown in Table 3.2. However, most of the interviewed companies appeared to have established technical centres in Korea out of a need to reduce production and logistics costs, thanks to their business ties with and proximity to Korean conglomerates such as Samsung and LG, rather than to develop original technologies and transfer know-how. Few companies experienced a transfer of know-how and even if there was such a transfer, it was a far cry from the transfer of key technologies since it focused on

Table 3.2 Reasons for having chosen Korea as the location for R&D centres

Company Name (Country)	Type of R&D Centre	Reasons
3M (USA)	Key Technical centre	Development capacity building
Hoya Electronics (Japan)	Applied technology centre	Technology and production management
AvanStrate (Japan)	Glass Substrate Production	Korea-specific R&D centre
Delphi (USA)	Tech Centre	Technology development base
Siemens Ultrasound (Germany)	Ultrasound Production and Development	Siemens ultrasound hub for the global market
Merck (Germany)	Advanced Technology Centre	R&D base
Kimberly-Clark (USA)	Innovative Technology Centre	Asia Pacific hub
Jenoptik (Germany)	Laser Application Centre	Asia Pacific hub
Bosch (Germany)	Technology Application Centre	New material development
Torayamk (Japan)	Advanced Material Research Centre	New material development

improvement of the existing products or production processes. Such discrepancies are more pronounced in Japanese companies. The key to research and development is strategic technology partnership between a parent company and an investment destination country; however, this study has revealed that most of the high-tech Japanese companies interviewed do not consider establishing a technology partnership with Korea, even though they have expanded their production lines over the years.

One of the striking findings of this study is that all the technologies listed in five patent applications filed by one of the interviewed Japanese companies over a period of five years in the early 2000s were developed in Japan. Such a case illustrates that there is a gap in the policy goal of attracting foreign investment with an eye to becoming a technology innovation powerhouse by attracting foreign R&D centres. For example, six out of the eight Japanese companies interviewed in this study, except for Torayamk and AvanStrate, did not have any plan to establish R&D centres for purposes of developing advanced original technologies in Korea. Furthermore, over half of the interviewed companies (automotive parts, lighting, LCD and others) seemed to view Korea as a cash cow; that is, a country with a low growth rate but highly profitable product growth rate. Except for very few, most of these companies are seriously considering China as a destination for their future R&D centres. In other words, Korea was not yet recognized by many foreign companies as a location for their R&D centres in Northeast Asia; rather it was seen as a production base for Asian markets. In particular, as has been shown in Table 3.3., the image of the Korean market perceived by every interviewed company (41 companies) was negative due to inconsistent policies and nationalism, as well as other factors, including a rigid labour market with high wages (100 per cent), the *Chaebol*'s monopoly (100 per cent) and saturated industries (automotive, lighting and others) (85 per cent). Moreover, only two companies (4.9 per cent) were of the opinion that Korea fitted the image of a R&D hub in

Table 3.3 Perceptions held by the interviewed companies* of Korea and its business environment

Areas	Yes (number of respondents)	% (%)
Rigid labour market	41	100
High wages	41	100
Chaebol's monopoly	41	100
Market saturation	35	85
Nationalism	30	73
Inconsistent policy	22	54
Political instability	12	29
Rampant corruption	5	12
Korea as an R&D hub in Northeast Asia	2	4.9

Note: *Interviewed foreign chambers of commerce in Korea are not included among the respondents in the table above.

Northeast Asia. Such national images have great implications for the government's policies in this regard.

The interview results in this study suggest the need for objective analyses of Korea's capabilities for technology development and of foreign high-tech companies' perceptions of the Korean market before establishing national development strategies focused on R&D. The negative images of the Korean market are potentially one of the risk factors that make many multinational companies choose other markets over Korea.[5]

Therefore, an investigation is urgently needed into the multinational companies which have already established R&D centres in Korea. Moreover, rather than analyzing abstract content, Korea's investment environment for R&D-driven foreign investment companies and the investment motivation should specifically be studied. It must be noted that the interviews in the present study yielded a substantially different result from the R&D characteristics by foreign investment companies in Korea. Differences are evident in responses to questions such as: What drives companies to establish R&D centres in Korea? Which business characteristics are more highly prioritized: research or development-related aspects? What progress has been made since entering the Korean market? What impact have these companies had on the Korean economy? A more detailed database needs to be built for each company; only then will more effective and efficient strategies be set to attract a greater number of foreign R&D centres.

The aspect of most concern highlighted above is the perception of a rigid labour market. The negative view of the Korean labour market seriously prevents foreign companies not only from investing in Korea but also from increasing investment or reinvesting. A globally renowned MNC said in the interview that the investment environment characterized by the rigid labour market and high wages had been one of the reasons why the CEO was against increasing investment/reinvesting in Korea. Another company was forced to put off its decision to reinvest in Korea due to a labour-management dispute in the year in which this interview was conducted (2010). These negative views have serious implications for Korea in attracting FDI and multinational company R&D centres. Furthermore, many foreign companies interviewed do not have accurate information on the Korean market. The interview findings indicate that over 55 per cent of the interviewed companies did not know that LG was a Korean company until they came to Korea. Some interviewees said they thought LG or Samsung was a Taiwanese company, showing a lack of awareness of the Korean key players in the global economy among non-Korean MNCs. Moreover, the 2017 survey conducted by the European Union Chamber of Commerce in Korea (EUCCK) reconfirms the interview findings of 2010 showing that doing international business in Korea has become harder (*The Business Times*, 2018). According to the EUCCK survey conducted with 108 company executives in November 2017, 79 (or 73.1 per cent) out of 108 companies indicated Korea's rigid labour market environment accompanied by rising labour costs as a key challenge, followed by ambiguous rules and regulations indicated by 69 per cent of the surveyed companies (*The Business Times*, 2018).

Is Korea's Gyeonggi province an attractive investment destination?

As mentioned earlier, one of the most important factors that helps conclude FDI deals is how attractive an investment destination Korea is to foreign investment companies, rather than simply the extent to which the government's policies are attractive. For MNCs, Korea is just one of many countries they consider for investment and ultimately, they choose a country with the most advantages. Foreign direct investment is made based on the assessment and analysis of market-ability and the market opportunities offered by an investment destination, as well as the current situation of the investment company. The policy environment of an investment destination, in other words its competitiveness in attracting investment, is considered after companies establish their 'entry-into-certain-market' strategies. Therefore, in the course of investigating whether Korea and in particular, Gyeonggi-do as the location of most MNCs R&D centres, is an ideal destination for foreign direct investment and has capabilities to play that role, an analysis of Gyeonggi-do and Korea should be made in terms of its appeal and competitiveness for foreign investment companies that are looking to establish a R&D centre or to start/expand their business.

This study has indicated that Gyeonggi-do has advantages in various areas which have favourably influenced the choices of foreign investment companies. The advantages include cheap land and rent, low-priced factory sites, easy market accessibility, easy accessibility to the production lines of conglomerates (easy accessibility to client companies–mostly among Japanese companies), and the benefits of an industrial complex dedicated to foreign companies. Moreover, one of Gyeonggi-do's major advantages in 2010 was its policy incentives such as investment inducement and promotion by the central or provincial government. In fact, as shown in Table 3.4., more than 95 per cent of the interviewed foreign investment companies (20 companies), which have invested in Gyeonggi-do, acknowledged the fact that the advantages of the province had influenced to a certain extent their decisions to make new investments or increase their investments. Furthermore, the interviews

Table 3.4 Reasons the interviewed companies (21 companies) gave for choosing Gyeonggi-do

List	No. of Companies	Percentage
Advantages: 　Easy access to the Seoul metropolitan area 　Industrial hub (cluster) 　Market accessibility 　Easy accessibility to client companies 　Easy accessibility to production lines	20	95
Site supports: 　Low land value and rent 　Low-priced factory site 　An industrial site dedicated to foreign companies	18	86

indicated that Gyeonggi-do's improvement measures to diversify foreign investment inducement, policy incentives and the aforementioned site supports, also played a substantial part in increasing investment from foreign investment companies.

As shown in Table 3.4, among the motivating factors leading to global companies setting up their R&D centres in Gyeonggi-do, location was the most attractive. An analysis of China, however, offers stark differences. More than 90 per cent of the interviewed companies (GSK, Delphi, Osram, Novartis, Bayer, Bosch and others) had already established several large-scale R&D centres in China by the mid or late-2000s. Certain pull factors according to interviewees may have been present, including the size of the economy, economic growth rate, a large pool of highly skilled workers, infrastructure and foreign R&D promotion policies such as massive financial packages at the national level. As was evident in the interviews conducted in this study, market size and potential presented by China were the most important factors encouraging foreign companies to choose China for investment. If the marketability of an investment destination is better than that of others, no matter how attractive other investment promotion policies are, they will not work. In that regard, the number of foreign R&D centres in Korea has been rapidly dropping since the mid-2000s, possibly due to far superior marketability and potential growth potential offered by China which have been rapidly rising since the 2000s.

It is clear that any R&D investment decisions or investment increases are dependent on changes in a company's value chain, as well as market structure, technological level, economy size, policy environment and a thorough understanding of the target market, which in other words means Return of Investment (ROI). The national policy incentives in the form of tax exemptions and reductions offered by an investment destination are just one of the considerations taken into account by foreign companies when making an investment decision, rather than a decisive factor.

As shown in Table 3.5., the investment environment of Korea is rapidly changing. Among all the interviewed companies (41 companies except for foreign chambers of commerce in Korea and Kim & Chang Law Firm), more than 66 per cent (27 companies) attributed the demand/technological level and importance of Korean conglomerates (with large global market shares in LCD/LED/IT and the automotive sector) to be the most decisive factor in choosing Korea for investment, while 46 per cent (19 companies) favoured the test bed function of the Korean market. Before the rise of China, the most decisive factor for choosing Korea was its market size and potential (34 per cent, 14 companies), followed by the companies' global strategies (24 per cent), securing a foothold in Northeast Asia (15 per cent) or exploration of a new market (15 per cent), which sheds light on how the investment environment of Korea has been changing. For example, all the interviewed Japanese companies (Takada, ECK, Jetco, Yoochang, Optical Daihen, AvanStrate, Mitsui, Hoya electronics and others) and European/US companies (Bosch, Delphi, UT Innovation, 3M, Merck, Siemens, Kimberly-Clark, Jenoptic and Osram) attributed the importance of the Korean market as the most decisive investment factor. Moreover, strategic partnership with Korean conglomerates (AvanStrate with Samsung, NCK with Hyundai,

Table 3.5 Reasons for investing in Korea

Reasons	No. of Companies	Percentage
Korean conglomerates' demand/ technology/share in the global market, the importance of Korean market	27	66
Korean market as a test bed	19	46
Market size / growth potentials	14	34
Part of the companies' globaliza- tion effort	10	24
Using it as a foothold in Northeast Asia	6	15
Exploration of a new market	6	15
Low wages	0	0

Mitsui with LG, Hoya Electronics with Samsung/LG, Merck with LG, and Yuhan Kimberly with Kimberly-Clark) was also mentioned as one of the decisive factors in choosing Korea for investment.

In the next part, we will look at the investment backgrounds of Siemens, a German company and Kimberly-Clark, a US company which established R&D centres in Bundang, Yongin and Gyeonggi-do, along with factors that affect foreign investment companies' decisions to invest in technology development and application centres in Gyeonggi-do.

Case study: Siemens Healthcare – Imaging and IT (Ultrasound)

Siemens is a Germany-based global company that focuses on energy products, automation systems and medical equipment, employing 450,000 people in 170 regional bases and networks all over the world. In 2002, it established a joint venture with K-Sonic and completed a medical ultrasound research centre in Sungnam city in 2003. In 2007, Siemens Medical Ultrasound division was launched and in 2008, it completed the construction of a production factory and a research centre in Pohang city, Gyeongbuk province in order to boost the development and production of ultrasound systems by investing USD 30 million. Currently, there are a total of about 500[6] Siemens employees in Korea involved in the production and research of ultrasound systems, including about 300 assembly-line workers, 50 office workers in procurement and marketing and 150 engineers in research and development. Siemens manufactures approximately 6,000 units of diagnostic apparatus and exports them to 170 countries, every year. Since 2010, Siemens Korea has become the Centre for Asia Growth in ultrasound systems and has played a leading role as the owner of Siemens' M3/4 market, by extension.

With regard to Siemens' outstanding growth in the Korean market, it is important to note that Siemens entered the Korean market in 2002 as part of the

M3/4 market strategies (interview conducted in Korea with Vice President of Siemens Korea Ultrasound System Division in 2010). The M3/4 market strategies are determined by the size and stable demand of a market that can complement generally low prices. In other words, an accurate understanding and forecast of growth potentials and changes in market demands would be critical to successful strategy implementation. For the last ten years, the high but sustainable profit generation and growth of Siemens Korea Ultrasound System Division not only have shown strong confidence in the potential of the Korean market, but have also helped maintain low-priced systems and given Siemens competitive advantages (low-priced products with high quality differentiation = customer satisfaction) through research and development.

Implications

The biggest driver of Siemens' success in the high-tech medical equipment market for ultrasound diagnostic systems is its unwavering confidence in the potential absorptive capacity (knowledge acquisition and assimilation) and real absorptive capacity (knowledge conversion and use) of its subsidiary and Korea. In other words, Siemens' confidence in the growth and innovative capability potentials of the Korean market has resulted in Korea becoming prime location for Siemens' research innovation of its ultrasound diagnostic systems as part of the strategy aimed at efficiently responding to a rapidly changing company, market and business environment. However, it was the human asset capacity available to Siemens and that could absorb Siemens' existing knowledge base in product innovation that helped support Siemens' unwavering confidence in the potential innovative capacity and that became the source of power that made Korea a true owner of the M3 market for ultrasound diagnostic systems (interview conducted in Korea with VP of Siemens Korea Ultrasound System Division in 2010). In addition, this level of success is the driving force for Siemens to engage in further R&D activities for ultrasound diagnostic systems in Korea.

Since the ultimate goal of inviting foreign R&D centres is the transfer of know-how and the resulting ripple effects, the Siemens case has very important implications. Moving its Centre for Excellence, currently located in California, USA, or transferring to an investment destination key people as part of a strategy for the localization and naturalization of executives in charge of technology management and production, gives rise to open innovation (value creation strategies by commercializing external or new technologies), leading to the transfer of original technologies and creating ripple effects which in turn will result in clinching future foreign investment deals. Moreover, at the moment when most of the mega multinational companies are either establishing or expanding their R&D centres in China, the expansion of Siemens Korea Ultrasound System Division (now promoted to being the headquarters for Siemens' global M3 market) is a very meaningful showing that Korea is a globally competitive investment destination that can be turned into a R&D base for multinational companies in certain areas. Although Siemens has established several R&D centres in China since 2007, when we interviewed with the VP of Siemens Korea Ultrasound Diagnostic System Division in person in 2015, the opinion was that China was no longer considered an ideal place to establish the Asian base for Siemens' ultrasound diagnostic systems in terms of R&D and production.

Case study 2: Kimberly-Clark Corporation – Innovation Centre Asia

Kimberly-Clark Corporation (hereafter referred to as KC Corporation) is a global US-based company, leading in healthcare and hygiene products (toilet paper, paper towels, tissues, female hygiene products, disposable diapers and special-purpose medical papers and other products) with sales of USD 20 billion in 2010 and employing 53,000 employees at its 150 offices in 42 countries around the world. In 1970, it launched a joint venture called Yuhan Kimberly Corporation with Yuhan. Since 2010, KC Corporation has established three Centres for Excellence, two of which are located in Wisconsin and Georgia respectively, and one, Innovation Centre Asia, established in Yongin, Gyeonggi-do in March 2007. The US-based R&D centres focus on corporate research and engineering, and innovation design, while the Korea-based R&D centre is dedicated to commercialization and globalization of products through close collaboration with the two US-based centres. In particular, although the Korea-based centre was established outside its home country and has a small number of employees (about 40 researchers in 2010), its establishment indicates that there has been a shift away from closed innovation which was limited to innovation undertaken by the internal R&D team, ranging from a long-term product design targeted at the global market, to product development and to product launch.

Based on the above, what are the implications of KC Corporation's experience for other multinational companies that plan to enter Asian markets; what are their motives and the significance of establishing centres for excellence, and what are the implications for Gyeonggi-do as a whole? As is the case for every other multinational company, innovation means a great deal to KC Corporation. Particularly, in the 2000s innovation for KC Corporation meant a major shift from the conventional corporate mindset, key capabilities and concept of R&D. In other words, the significance of the Centre for Excellence in Yongin indicates that there has been a shift from closed innovation strategy (a strategy led by the internal R&D team to respond to changes in product longevity, market environment, service and process) centred on the North American market, which KC Corporation long held onto until the early 2000s, to open innovation strategy (a value creation strategy with commercialization of outside or new technologies). The scope of R&D activities undertaken by foreign R&D centres in Korea are often limited to closed innovation. In contrast, Innovation Centre Asia established in Yongin engages in open innovation, based on technology partnership and a win-win strategy by using its pool of highly skilled workers. Furthermore, the centre has particular significance as the first global R&D centre established by KC Corporation outside the US. Such a shift to open innovation has been driven by market maturity or saturation in the US and South American markets, which in turn resulted in a need to explore new markets, develop new products and differentiate key capabilities with respect to the general characteristics and buying traits of the global market and consumers. With a close innovation strategy which relies on the headquarters having complete control over an entire process of the value chain starting from product production, design, marketing and launch (logistics), consistent with the corporate vision of developing all the technologies needed by the company in house, KC Corporation realized that it could not survive in an increasingly competitive global market. This realization has led the company to shift to an open innovation strategy since the mid-2000s and has motivated the company to make inroads into new markets such as Asia (interview conducted in Korea with the Global Director of KC Innovation Centre Asia in 2010).

Implications

As has been discussed earlier in the case study of Siemens, foreign direct investment is made on the basis of a region or market. After KC Corporation decided to explore new markets in Asia, widespread market research was conducted on different markets for two years between 2005 and 2006. The markets investigated by the company included Korea along with Japan, China, Singapore and India. There are two major reasons for KC Corporation choosing Korea. The first reason is the brand awareness and value of Yuhan Kimberly, and the second reason is the success Yuhan Kimberly has had in the Korean market and the other Asian markets. In other words, the brand awareness and value of a company (Yuhan Kimberly) or a region (Gyeonggi-do) have become a driving force for further investment. In addition, as with Siemens, KC Company's strong confidence in the Korean market's capacity for innovation, its availability of human assets and their capacity led to its decision to establish its Centre for Excellence in Korea.

KC Company employs about 40 people in 2010 in its Yongin R&D centre, their hard work for the last three years has resulted in the R&D centre's successful operations. This success, in turn, indicates that its Yongin centre has proved its mettle and potentials to be part of KC Company's corporate research team focused on long-term research, and by extension, to become a true innovation centre for the company. As such, the centre will go down in the company's history as a good case for an open business model that proves not only that Korea is an ideal place to implement the open innovation strategy introduced in the mid-2000s, but also that such a move can lead to the transfer of original technologies and the ripple effects of technology in the domestic market.

Interview Results

The following are the results of this study based on the interviews with the MNCs conducted in Korea in 2010.

- The purpose of foreign R&D centres established in Korea by most of foreign investment companies was to supply parts and materials to Korean conglomerates (Samsung, Hyundai and LG), not to do research and development/engineering.

- There was a large technological gap in the effect of transferring key technologies which is the original purpose of attracting foreign R&D centres.
- The relatively affordable human assets of Korea which are an absolute advantage over China, were the decisive factor in the establishment of foreign R&D centres in Korea.
- Korea's strategy to become the R&D hub for Northeast Asia initiated by the Roh administration is not feasible. Companies viewed the idea of establishing Centres for Excellence in Korea in a negative light and underestimate Korea's capacity for research and development.
- Gyeonggi-do's locational advantages (low land value and rents, low-priced factory site, easy market accessibility, easy accessibility to client companies and production lines, benefits of an industrial site dedicated to foreign companies) have been one of the factors in the investment/investment expansion decisions of foreign investment companies.
- From a R&D perspective, the brand image of Gyeonggi-do was then poor and needed overall improvement.

As has been confirmed by the case studies of Siemens and Kimberly-Clark and the interviews, the most significant reason for foreign companies having chosen Korea to establish their R&D bases was the country's global investment advantages, such as the possibility of using cost-effective, outstanding R&D human assets, marketability and geopolitical competitiveness as a mediator between the Japanese and Chinese markets.

Moreover, the locational advantages specific to Gyeonggi-do played a substantial part in attracting investors. The aforementioned two case studies prove that Korea is competitive enough to be a developed country's outsourcing destination. This point was proven by the technology development centres established in Gyeonggi-do by Bosch, a world-renowned German automotive parts maker, Jenoptik, a laser material processing company and Merck, a global LCD top seller, all of which took part in this study.

Nonetheless, in spite of these numerous competitive and locational advantages, some of the issues this study has pointed out need to be addressed immediately in order to maximize the effects of foreign R&D centres established in Gyeonggi-do and Korea. Given the reality where investment-related decisions are made by a few people in a company, the image of Gyeonggi-do was a critical determinant of investment decisions made by foreign companies. One of the key interview questions was how well foreign investment companies had known Gyeonggi-do and Korea before investment. To our surprise, most of the interviewed companies knew nothing about Gyeonggi-do. Of course, this is partly due to the short history of implementing investment promotion policies when considering investment destinations. Nevertheless, this observation proves the point that Korea was not perceived as a brand by many foreign companies, thus showing the limits of its brand strategies. When foreign companies think of Gyeonggi-do and Korea, what comes to mind first? What efforts has Gyeonggi-do and Korea been making to build its brand in order to attract foreign investors? In addition, what are the correlations between its effort and its track record of attracting foreign direct investment? How has Gyeonggi-do and Korea been branding its global and locational advantages? How much influence do such branding strategies have on an investment environment? For example, 'Global Inspiration', Gyeonggi-do's brand slogan in 2010, appears to have had very weak correlations with the effort of attracting foreign R&D centres. It would have been more effective to create a slogan that promoted Gyeonggi-do's competitive advantages, such as a substantial pool of human assets, high-quality educational environment and location of Korea's industrial and IT hub. For Gyeonggi-do and Korea to rise as a R&D hub, the province needs to be attractive and appealing to foreign investment companies. In this study, we have found that grandiose incentives and brand slogans will not make Gyeonggi-do and Korea suddenly attractive to foreign investment companies for their R&D centre location. Potential high-tech investors are attracted by real success stories of foreign companies in Gyeonggi-do and Korea. We believe transparent, realistic and honest promotional strategies focusing on Korea and Gyeonggi-do's pivotal role and support in the establishment and successful operations of multinationals' global R&D centres, and its continuous investment service and follow-ups for investment companies, will resonate better with foreign companies. Therefore, it is time that measures were taken to make comprehensive branding strategies that can most effectively appeal to foreign investment companies, employing various channels, including investment and trade bureaus, economic policy departments, policymaking divisions, and heads of foreign investment companies, in particular German, US and Japanese, chairmen of foreign chambers of commerce in Korea (American Chamber of Commerce, AMCHAM Korea and EUCCK).

As a result, this book proposes the creation of a branding team which is comprised of the CEOs of foreign investment companies that are successfully operating in Korea and Gyeonggi-do. It would be more effective for product users to promote Korea, rather than product makers, to attract foreign investment.

Furthermore, Korea needs to build a competitive system through which relevant stakeholders can engage in close and sustainable collaboration and cooperation to understand the operations and the current status of successful R&D centres in Korea and Gyeonggi do, as well as a very detailed database of foreign investment companies. In particular, if the Comprehensive Investment Promotion Plan for Gyeonggi-do released in September 2010 was to become a real turning point rather than a set of superficial activities to promote growth, strategies were needed to be implemented to attract and utilize foreign investment companies qualitatively by building and analyzing a detailed and thorough database of the foreign investment companies in Gyeonggi-do. This study proposes the creation of a team within Korean and the Gyeonggi provincial government dedicated to analyzing and strategizing the businesses of foreign investment companies in Gyeonggi-do and Korea. The team's activities should be recorded in detail and up-to-date information and analysis of foreign investment companies should be shared. In other words, a highly detailed database should be built indicating which area foreign investment companies focus on or prioritize; for example, research and development, as opposed to what their business performance has been in Korea, or how their performance has affected Korea's or Gyeonggi-do's economic performance. Furthermore, government policies should also be complemented in order to establish, grow and maintain the ties with foreign investment companies.

There is also a need to change the way we equate a new foreign investment with success. So far, we have witnessed numerous cases of MNCs entering the Korean market but soon abandoning their businesses or moving their investment to a third country. It is a well-known fact that there has not yet been a systematic investigation of these companies and a root cause analysis of such outcomes. In fact, foreign R&D centres are just the beginning of a long-term success (e.g. transfer of original technology, naturalization of a parent company). Do Korea and Gyeonggi-do still maintain the commitment and stance which they had before clinching foreign investment deals? The interviews with foreign investment companies located in Korea and Gyeonggi-do area indicate a negative answer to this question. As has been said earlier in this chapter, only two out of all the interviewed companies were positive about Korea's potential to become the R&D centre for Northeast Asia. Such a response is indicative of the fact that it is still too early for Korea to be perceived as a global technology powerhouse. One of the most frequent questions many of the interviewed companies said they had been asked by the Gyeonggi provincial office was in relation to the possibility of an investment increase or an investment expansion. This fact shows that the provincial government is more interested in increasing the foreign investment volume, than realizing the original purpose of attracting foreign R&D centres, which is to complement Korea's small capacity for innovation and to upgrade its industrial structure.

This book attributes the aforementioned misplaced perception of foreign investment to an absence of systematic data. It is time that Korea understood that foreign investment can prove to be a curse in disguise if follow-up actions are not properly taken, including response measures made from a detailed analysis of the development and implementation of strategies to attract foreign investment and to maximize its ripple effects.

More attention needs to be paid to the fact that the entrepreneurial interest in investing and support from the central and provincial governments are as important as policy support in clinching an investment deal.

Conclusion

The qualitative in-depth interviews substantiate the view that Korea is looking to the next decade and beyond, and that the country will continue to grapple with the challenges of improving its nation image in the face of increasing competition globally. While the interview results in this study are based on earlier fieldwork conducted in Korea in 2010, they still seem to be valid currently in 2018 given that the negative images of the Korean market even today are often regarded as one of the risk factors that make many MNCs choose other markets over Korea (*The Business Times*, 2018). The data shows that the collective nature of economic nationalism (i.e. market access barriers in the form of regulations/rules against foreign businesses in Korea) mobilized by the state is still perceived by MNCs as prevalent in Korea despite the rapid development of globalization and cosmopolitanism. Hence, what dominant shape Korea's competitiveness will take in the future to be successfully integrated into the global economy will not only depend on domestic industries and economic policies, together with political maturity so that the country is able to develop and sustain its global competitiveness, but to what extent the country will be able to improve and reshape its image as a difficult market for international business.

Notes

1 The key actions prescribed by the IMF to be taken in the Korean economy included:
   - Fiscal adjustments that would include adjustments of the current account, redress of earlier public sector excesses and the guarantee of a correction of private sector excesses without unduly compressing domestic demand;
   - Firm monetary policy;
   - Restructuring of weak financial sectors, closure of insolvent institutions, strengthening of regulations and supervision; and
   - Improved public and corporate governance, and increased transparency and accountability

2 Korea's post-independence industrial capitalism has had a long history of EN, stimulated initially by negative experiences as a result of earlier interactions with foreign regimes, then by a desperate necessity for economic survival.

3 For a comprehensive discussion of globalization in East Asia, see Jomo (2003); Alden, Steenkamp and Batra (2006).

4 In the initial period of Korea's modern economic growth during the 1960s, the inflow of foreign capital was encouraged to make up for a shortage of domestic savings and foreign reserves. However, the Korean government preferred foreign borrowing, which brought foreign resources under its control, over IFDI. The general fear of Korean industries being dominated by foreign entities, which was deeply rooted in Korea's then-recent history of Japanese colonization (1910–1945), was too widespread for the government to accommodate foreign management.

5 The result of an interview with Mr. Jean-Jacques Gauhar, the chairman of the EU Chamber of Commerce in Korea.

6 This figure is greater than the number of employees Siemens employs in California, USA.

Part III
Branding Korea

4 Korea and its nation brand

Introduction

The growing interest in the field of nation branding continues unabated to this day, from both academics as well as public and private organizations (Anholt, 2006, 2008; Browning, 2015; Dinnie, 2016; Gupta, Foroudi, Väätänen, Gupta, and Tiu Wright, 2018; Kerr and Wiseman, 2013; Rasmussen and Merkelsen, 2012). In their book *Diplomacy in a Globalizing World: Theories and Practices*, Kerr and Wiseman (2013: 354) define nation branding as 'the application of corporate marketing concepts and techniques to countries, in the interests of enhancing their reputation in international relations.' This image enhances the country's marketability and serves as a source of influence as nations engage in bilateral or multi-lateral trade and diplomacies, and is the new currency as countries realize that soft power can be as forceful, if not more, than the hard power that has evidently failed in many instances.

Beyond its seemingly straight forward definition, the concept of nation brand may itself be paradoxical in a globalized world and mired in complexity as the concept is rooted across multiple disciplines including cultural sociology (Browning, 2015), national security (Rasmussen and Merkelsen, 2012), public policy and administration (Gilboa, 2008), and marketing (Anholt, 2008; O'Shaughnessy and O'Shaughnessy, 2000). For example, Kerr and Wiseman (2013), among others (Browning, 2015; Rasmussen and Merkelsen, 2012), focus on nation branding as a mechanism to enhance a country's cultural and political influence in the world, as an attractive nation brand would allow the country to have its voice heard in international affairs. In contrast, others look to nation branding to improve a country's economic vitality as a successful nation brand image plays a pivotal role in enticing investment capital, increasing exports and attracting inbound tourists (Anholt, 2007; Fan, 2006; K.-T. Lee, Lee and Lee, 2014; Zeugner-Roth, Žabkar and Diamantopoulos, 2015). From this perspective, the concept of nation branding is related to economic nationalism, whereby the interests of the state and corporate enterprises are entrenched. An attractive nation brand helps to draw in foreign investments, skilled labour, tourists and international students, as well as import-export trade by boosting the competitiveness of the nation's enterprises.

In short, a nation brand is a multidimensional collection of elements, including people, culture, history, geography, well-known personalities and products that projects a perceived image in the minds of international stakeholders. Through association with these elements, a nation brand is etched in people's memory as it evolves slowly over time. The multidimensional structure of a nation brand also implies that it is difficult, if not impossible, to craft a single message or image that can appeal to a wide international audience. Naturally, stereotyping, media coverage or even personal experience has significant bearings on the image formation and once formed, it takes considerable effort to change it.

Korea's government initiatives on nation brand building

While a nation brand image can exist without conscious effort by a nation or its people, more often than not, governments make a concerted effort to positively shape this image as part of their international engagements. Indeed, some have asserted that nation branding must inevitably be a responsibility of, or at least fervently supported by, a country's government. As Anholt (2008: 23, emphasis in the original) puts it, nation branding is necessarily 'a *component of national policy*, never a "campaign" that is separate from planning, governance, or economic development'.

In the history of modern Korea, nation branding can be traced back to efforts by then leader, General Park Chung-hee, shortly following the Korean War (1950–1953) in early attempts to kick start the development of Korea toward becoming a globally competitive capitalist economy. Park's political legitimacy – some would even argue his justification for the military coup that brought him to power (Schwak, 2016) – rested upon his promise of *Jokuk Kundaewha* (조국근대화), the modernization and transformation of the fatherland into a world-class nation. Implicit in the discourse was the acceptance that Korea, at that time, was ranked low among nations that were in fierce competition with one another (Lie, 1998). Successive governments have continued the legacy of modernizing Korea by shaping its nation brand image. One notable example is President Kim Young-Sam's 1993 reformation policy of *Segyehwa* (세계화), which institutionalized not only Korea's economic liberalization efforts through international trade, but also the embracing of cultural understanding and social open-mindedness towards other nations (S. S. Kim, 2000). This reform aimed to prepare Korea to meet challenges in its globalization journey.

However, as successive governments gained awareness of the lag between Korea's global image and its economic success, it becomes clear that much work is still necessary in advancing a positive image of Korea to the world. As recently as 2006, people were still unaware of the origin of Samsung and often mistook it to be a Japanese company (Analytics, 2006). A 2009 study published by the Korea Trade Investment Promotion Agency similarly found that Westerners associated Korea with the nuclear crisis in North Korea, and that the majority of Americans (64 per cent) could not correctly identify the origin of Samsung, arguably the most famous of all Korean brands (cited in Ih-Prost and Bondaz, 2014). Preceding this study by the Korea Trade Investment Promotion Agency, the oft-referenced Anholt-GfK Nation Brands Index had reported a constant downgrading of Korea's nation image from 2005 (25th position) to 2008 (33rd position).

Obviously, such negative perceptions have not gone unnoticed nor the importance of a favourable nation brand image ignored. An early attempt to formally institutionalize governmental efforts to manage Korea's nation brand image was the formation of the National Image Committee during the administration of President Kim Dae-jung (1998–2003). The fact that the committee was chaired by the President signalled the policy importance of this institution.

The committee was later superseded by the Presidential Council on Nation Branding under the supervision of President Lee Myung-bak's government as efforts continued to improve, or at least reverse the deficit of, brand 'Korea'. Acknowledging that Korea was disadvantaged economically as well as in global politics by an unfavourable nation brand image, President Lee formed the Council in 2009 to spearhead and coordinate all nation branding initiatives by public and private enterprises. As a top-level public office overseeing all government efforts to promote the improvement of brand 'Korea', the Council played several roles. It enacted policies and set up a system to manage and coordinate activities across all ministries. The primary goal of the Council was to raise Korea's status by gaining credibility and likeability on the global stage by contributing to the international community and helping Koreans become responsible and global citizens. The premise of these efforts was that raising respect for Korea will inevitably also support Korean businesses and nationals abroad (PCNB, 2009). To be specific, the Council formulated a five-pronged strategy to increase the nation's brand value: (1) contribute to the international community, (2) embrace multiculturalism and be receptive to foreign culture, (3) become responsible global citizens, (4) promote modern technology and products, and (5) portray an appealing culture, thereby attracting tourists.

Since its 2009 inception, the Council has hosted numerous Korea Week events abroad, including in Indonesia, Vietnam, India, China, Kazakhstan and France, as a form of cultural exchange in order to showcase Korea. During this period, Korea has also hosted the 2010 G20 Summit, the 2012 Nuclear Security Summit, the 2012 World Expo and the 2017 Winter Olympics, all of which are high profile efforts that have boosted the country's image in the eyes of the global community.

Importantly, the Council held the view that the improvement of Korea's nation brand would help promote Korean products and services abroad. In this regard, the Council aimed to act as a catalyst to strengthen the partnership between the government and private sectors. To promulgate this intention, the Council was deliberately made up of civilian business experts and ministers, with civilians forming the majority.

The Council was subsequently dismantled in 2013 when President Park Geun-hye (2013–2017) came to power, at which time Korea had achieved significant progress in its nation brand image. The frequently referenced Anholt-GfK Nation Brands Index ranked Korea in 31st position at the start of President's Lee Myung-bak's Presidential Council on Nation Branding in 2009. Korea has since seen its rank on the index climb to 27th position in 2011 and further improve to 15th position globally in 2013. Thus far, under the watch of President Moon Jae-in (May 2017 to present), the Council or an equivalent body has not been reinstated.

As Korea's nation brand image improves, the country is enjoying the immediate and important benefit of gaining greater soft power for public diplomacy internationally. A favourable nation brand image is tied to Korea's ability to build and maintain positive relationships with other countries, thereby enlarging its sphere of influence in public diplomacy (Browning, 2015; Kinsey and Chung, 2013; Ma, Song and Moore, 2012). Arguably, in the present climate, no other benefit is more important for Korea than fostering a mutually peaceful and respectful relationship with its northern neighbour (Jonsson, 2006; Padden, 2018).

Nation brand and cultural diplomacy

However, effective nation branding is not confined to public propaganda efforts to boost economic activities or for public diplomacy; it also depends on different stakeholders collaborating in harmony to send a consistently believable message to the intended audiences (Dinnie, Melewar, Seidenfuss and Musa, 2010; Kinsey and Chung, 2013). Hong (2014) contends that during the process of developing a nation brand, a national cultural identity is simultaneously created, one that becomes internalized by the public. This is analogous to what some have called cultural diplomacy, where culture becomes a soft resource that is applied by the government to advance national interests (Ahearne, 2009; Kang, 2015). In other words, a nation branding agenda can be melded with a cultural agenda to reinforce national image identity internally and externally. Similarly, for Korea nation branding is a direct outcome of a country's cultural policy (Kang, 2015; Yim, 2002). To this end, the Ministry of Foreign Affairs and Trade (MOFAT) specified that along with the focus on defence in the 1980s and economic and trade focus in the 1990s, culture will be the third pillar of the country's diplomatic power in the twenty-first century (MOFAT, 2010).

Korea's strong cultural identity, which stems from the nation's past and present, and is being projected into the future, serves to bond fellow nationals. This sense of belonging helps foster a close link between an individual self and the collective Korean society. Similar to culture, cultural identity embodies characteristics of the people that are reflexively stable. Consequently, any changes in this identity must be accompanied by fundamental shifts in the country's political, economic and cultural fabric. Indeed, as Eckert et al. (1990) pointed out in their book *Korea, Old and New: A History*, modern Korean cultural nationalism is rooted in the nation's remarkably homogeneous culture as the unified Korean race or *Han minjok* (한민족). It is for this reason that multiculturalism is not considered in Korean cultural policies (Yim, 2002).

However, Korea's cultural identity suffered from early events including Japanese colonialism (1910–1945), the Korean War (1950–1953) and the division of the Korean peninsula. The cultural erosion is also a consequence of the nation's rapid modernization, which brings along with it an indiscriminate influx of Western culture. Hence, even as early as the first Korean republic (1948–1960) headed by President Rhee Syngman, the development of a national culture had gained importance and recognition. This direction was further cemented during the 18-year reign

(1961–1979) of President Park Chung-hee. While President Park recognized the value of linking Korea's national image with its traditional ethnic heritage, he also realized that aligning the national identity with traditional culture could create a nation image of cohesion and unity. This would then serve the broad political agenda of legitimizing his regime, as well as rebuilding the Korean identity after the devastations of the Japanese occupation (1910–1945) and then the Korean War (1950–1953) (Kang, 2015; H.-K. Lee, 2013; Yim, 2002). In particular, the administration of President Park published the first five-year (1974–1979) master plan for cultural development, although the scope of the plan narrowly focused on folk art and traditional culture.

Successive administrations until the present day have continued to pursue cultural policies to sustain the nation's cultural image. For example, rather than limited to folk and traditional arts, President Chun Doo Hwan (1980–1988) extended public support to contemporary art and to the everyday life of the people.[1] President Roh Tae-woo's government (1988–1993) established a ten-year plan with the motto 'Culture for All the People' and the primary goal of establishing a strong cultural identity through the promotion of arts and culture. Later, President Kim Dae-jung (1998–2003) introduced the New Cultural Policy – essentially an update of the cultural policy at the time of the previous administration – that articulated a more 'industrial and scientific' approach in exporting the Korean culture. Cultural diplomacy had gained full recognition of its importance in shaping Korea's international image and reputation. The Basic Law for Cultural Industry Promotion passed in 1999 to accompany that New Cultural Policy stipulated that the government would develop and support the cultural industry with the *segyehwa* (세계화) reformation policy. Such initiatives that see unilaterally direct involvements by institutional players to build nation image is referred to by Kang (2015) as 'explicit' cultural diplomacy. For example, the Ministry of Culture and Sports (MCS) established the Top Ten Symbols of Korean Culture, and then aggressively promoted them through various PR activities via overseas government channels (MCS, 1996). The ten symbols that strongly represent Korean heritage are as follows:

- The traditional outfit, *hanbok* (한복)
- The alphabet system, *hangul* (한글)
- Traditional food, kimchi (김치) and *bulgogi* (불고기)
- Buddhist temples, Bulguksa (불국사) and Seokgulam (경주 석굴암)
- The martial art form, taekwondo (태권도)
- The medicinal herb, ginseng or Insam (인삼)
- The traditional mask dance, Talchum (탈춤)
- The royal ancestral shrine, Jongmyo (종묘)
- The national park of Mount Seoraksan (설악산)
- Korean artists of international calibre

Although the list was subsequently expanded under President Roh Moo-hyun's (2003–2008) administration to one hundred items, ostensibly to broaden and modernize the succession of Korean traditional culture, the primary objective of such a list remains unchallenged: cultural diplomacy through concerted and explicit institutional actions are instrumental in shaping Korea's international image.

Indeed, this strategy of tying nation brand building to culture is not new. Other countries have taken similar approaches. When the former Yugoslavia broke up in the early 1990s, each breakaway republic was left to fend for itself in terms of building a distinct national identity. Slovenia systematically adopted the slogan 'Feel S*love*nia', emphasizing the '*love*' in order to engender feelings of attachment and a sense of pride among native Slovenes, as well as to target international tourism, thereby creating a national identity (Volcic, 2008). Likewise, Merrilees, Miller, Ge and Tam (2018) suggest that the perceived brand of Hong Kong can be shaped through associating the city with integral cultural values, specifically its Confucian background, intangible cultural heritage, as well as its material lifestyle activities, such as its eateries.

Hanryu (한류) as cultural diplomacy

As opposed to explicit actions by the government, nation branding can also occur by enlisting different stakeholders to collaborate in harmony to send a consistently believable message to the intended audiences (Dinnie et al., 2010; Kinsey and Chung, 2013). This includes requiring citizens to live and even promulgate the desired brand image through their cultural identity; take Israel's 2010 'Making the Case for Israel' for example. Through the campaign, the Israeli government urged its citizens to act like diplomats while travelling abroad, to counter negative perceptions about the country following its one-sided war against Hamas in Gaza. Television advertisements themed 'Are you fed up with the way we are portrayed around the world? You can change the picture', urged citizens to help spread the message that Israel is modern, sophisticated and peace-loving. To facilitate this, brochures that provided positive statistics and claims were distributed by airlines. Consistent with this approach of enlisting original citizens in nation building, a proposed action of the Presidential Council on Nation Branding was to send 3,000 Koreans as brand ambassadors abroad to promote Korean culture, although it is not clear whether this initiative was successfully executed.

Korean nation brand building is also occurring through implicit cultural diplomacy using activities such as international cultural exchanges of artistic performances. This neo-liberal approach by the Korean government to share nation branding responsibility with the populace is no less apparent than in the cultural expansionism of Korea's pop culture. This soft approach that has allowed Korea to reimage itself is fuelled by the mass consumption of popular Korean culture, thereby resulting in the formation of specific images and perceptions of the country and its people.

Indeed, in a study on identifying the representative factors that underpinned Korea's nation brand, Kinsey and Chung (2013) found that Korean pop culture, alongside historical and cultural factors, did have an influence on the formation of the country's image. Purportedly coined by the media to describe the rapid diffusion of Korean entertainment and culture overseas, the *Hanryu* (한류) neo-logism of K-pop and K-drama clearly has had an impact on improving the coun-try's image and products, first within the Asia Pacific region and later in the Middle East, the US, Europe and even South America (Cha and Kim, 2011; Y. Y. Cho, 2012; Ryoo, 2009). It is simply too hard to ignore the fact that Psy's Gangnam Style video, viewed more than three billion times on YouTube (see www.youtube.com/watch?v=9bZkp7q19f0 published at the time this book went to press) does help shape outsiders' perceptions of Korea.

The influence of the entertainment media on a country's image has been well-documented in the literature of advertising, brand management and retailing (Gupta et al., 2018; Jang, 2018; Mikhailitchenko, Javalgi, Mikhailitchenko, and Laroche, 2009; O'Connor and Bolan, 2008). By familiarizing the audience with a certain country through visual scenes, such entertainment videos are highly effec-tive in stimulating foreigners' interests in and impressions of the country, includ-ing those who have yet to set foot in the country. In their study on the effectiveness of various information sources for promoting a travel destination image, Govers, Go and Kumar (2007) found that perceptions of a country stem-med more from vicarious sources, such as movies containing scenes of the country or personalities associated with the country, rather than from overt advertising and promotion.

In other words, *Hanryu* (한류) is not just entertainment. As a form of cultural nationalism, the concept is a 'soft power' tool for public and political diplomacy (Kinsey and Chung, 2013; Ma et al., 2012; Porteux and Choi, 2018). As *Hanryu* spreads infectiously through the region, the Korean government is quick to capi-talize on this phenomenon by aiding Korean media industries in exporting Korean pop culture in order to enhance the country's national image. In particular, Pre-sident Lee Myung-bak's (2008–2013) Presidential Council on Nation Branding (대통령기록) explicitly recognized the key roles that *Hanryu* plays in contributing to the nation's image building effort within the international community.

Observers generally concur that the popularity of *Hanryu* is due to the ability of the Korean culture to serve as a bridge between Western and Asian cultures. *Hanryu* is able to morph Western culture in a form that is palatable to Asian audiences whose background and ethos are more similar to Korea than to the West (Hogarth, 2013; Ryoo, 2009). Cha and Kim (2011) similarly contend that the driving force behind the rapid expansion of *Hanryu* lies in the 'glocalization' of Korean popular culture, where the local culture is thoroughly infused with the global trend. Such cultural expansionism no doubt plays a crucial role in shaping the outside view of Korea. For example, Lee, Ham and Kim (2015) demonstrated in an empirical study that Korean celebrities had a strong and direct influence on how people in four countries (Hong Kong, Bangkok, Sydney and Dubai) per-ceived Korea. The more the people liked the celebrities, the higher they rated the country image of Korea. Similarly, in a study on identifying the representative factors that underpinned Korea's nation brand, Kinsey and Chung (2013) found that besides historical and cultural factors, Korean pop culture also had an influ-ence on the formation of the country's image.

Ironically, the link between *Hanryu* and Korea's diplomacy in international affairs has its shortcomings, as exemplified by the recent case of China banning the appearance of Korean celebrities on Chinese television. Ostensibly, the act was a retaliation following the Korean government's decision to allow the deployment of the Terminal High Altitude Area Defence (THAAD) system on the Korean peninsula by the US in order to deter potential threats from North Korea.

Hanryu, as a diplomatic tool, may also have gone too far in some instances, such as the aforementioned, as popularly reported by various Korean media at the time. Nonetheless, this incident further illustrates the pervasiveness of *Hanryu* outside Korea:

> When President Roh Moo Hyun invited Vietnamese Prime Minister Phan Van Khai and his delegation for a luncheon meeting last September, something unexpected happened. After a moment of calm, the Vietnamese officials stood up one by one and started to line up in front of a woman, asking her to sign their menus. The woman was actress Kim Hyun Joo, heroine of the SBS TV drama *Glass Shoes* (유리구두), which had been shown on Vietnamese television in May 2003. The actress had become well-known in Vietnam after the drama became a big hit there. The commotion settled down only after a Korean general promised the actress's autographs for everyone after lunch. The centre of attention during the luncheon apparently was not President Roh or Prime Minister Khai, but the actress, Kim, showing that perhaps the 'Korean Wave' is stronger than diplomacy.
>
> Korean Wave Crashes on Asian Shores (www.korea.net), 25 August, 2004

Conclusion

To conclude this chapter, it can be said that Korea has come a long way from the war-torn days of the Korean War (1950–1953). Over the past four decades, Korea has traversed a steep ascent to become a global economic powerhouse, the eleventh largest in the world currently. The rise has been accompanied by a peaceful transition to a more liberal democracy compared to the early post-war days when the authoritarian ruling party was backed by the military force. Despite its economic success and efforts by the Korean government, along with private enterprises, to improve its nation brand image, it seems that more work is needed. The West still views Korea as an impoverished nation. Schröter and Schwekendiek (2015) recently reported that the German media still associate Korea with negative images including being unsafe, corrupt and unstable. It also does not help that the antics of North Korea and its leaders continue to cast shadows on Korea as a whole, thereby undercutting the democratic South's efforts to build a more favourable image particularly with Western audiences (Kinsey and Chung, 2013). Another relevant example of the above is that as recently as 2006, there still was a lack of awareness of Samsung's origins which were mistakenly believed to be Japanese (Analytics, 2006).

Regardless of these possibly isolated incidents, the nation's brand image has clearly lent, and will continue to lend, a helping hand to boost the competitiveness of the Korean economy. In the next chapter, we will further explore this issue by tracing the progress of Korea's industrialization and how it impacts its nation brand image.

Note

1 Later in 1993, when President Kim Young Sam formulated his *segyehwa* (세계화) policies, it was recognised that nation brand building efforts were inextricably linked to individual Koreans readjusting their social norms and attitudes towards foreign culture (S. S. Kim, 2000).

5 The impact of Korea's industrialization on nation brand

Korea's industrialization, late particularly by Western timelines, kick started in earnest in the early 60s, joined by the formation of the *Chaebol*, to spear head large scale export-oriented industrialization. According to a recent report by Deloitte (GMCI, 2016), Korea's manufacturing industry accounted for about 86 per cent of total merchandise exports. The country has come a long way since immediately after Korean Wars (1950–1953) when manufacturing accounted for a mere 12 per cent of GDP to about 30 per cent by 2017. But the industrialization objectives and characteristics, articulated in successive five-year plans under different administrations, vastly differ during the early post-war days to the recent times.

The early years

Korea was predominantly an agricultural economy until the Korean War. Initially (in the early 1960s), the government's import substitution policies were aimed to make Koreans self-reliant while increasing their wealth (Chung, 1974), although some have argued that the approach was a mistake (e.g. see Harvie and Lee, 2003). By implementing successive five-year plans, the Korean government systemically enacted import substitution policies through tariffs and subsidies, as well as through regulations and restrictions on foreign investments and technology transfers in order to develop strong local companies that were capable of competing internationally. The omnipresence of the state in guiding and even regulating private industries benefitted major family-owned *Chaebol* as major financial resources and coveted public infrastructure projects were channelled to them. In turn, the *Chaebol* invested heavily in R&D that would eventually bring about world-class brands including the likes of Samsung and Hyundai (Shin, 2005). The characteristics of the country's industrialization process are long considered as one that is underpinned by political nationalism (Chey and Helleiner, 2018; Kim, 2018).

As the early industrialization period focused on industries such as textile and garment manufacturing, and supplying components to Japanese electronics manufacturers, the prevailing nation brand image at that time was one associated with mediocre, low-technology, light-manufacturing and low-value products. It was therefore not surprising that Korean exports were generally not well regarded. Then came the period of the late 1960s to 1970s, when the country shifted towards heavy industries, first in steel production and then in steel consuming sectors such as shipbuilding and heavy machineries. This period would come to be known for its heavy and chemical industries (HCI) drive. For example, Hyundai, originally an engineering and construction company, diversified into ship building at this time. This heavy industry image would later help launch Korean cars, which enjoyed government protection through high tariffs on imported cars. Notably, Hyundai Motors mass-produced Korea's first car, the *Pony*, in 1975 and began exporting it the following year, starting with South America before expanding to Europe. Harbouring an image of a skilled workforce, Korean industrial exports extended to machines and tools. The change in industrial structure from primary to secondary is typical of developing countries, but the rate of change occurred much quicker in Korea compared to other developing countries at a similar stage in their industrialization process (Chung, 1974; Cole and Lyman, 1971). During this period, Korea had begun to shed its image as a low-cost original equipment manufacturer (OEM) of low-technology products and had transformed itself into a competitive heavy industry force. Interestingly, this metamorphosis of the Korean brand image occurred at a time when traditional Western industrial giants, particularly the UK, were in decline.

As indicated in earlier parts of this book, Korea's rapid success of capitalist industrialization should also be attributed to the Korean government's initiatives and creation of special economic zones (SEZ) in the 1970s. These zones, which offered one-stop shop processing of import/export customs procedures and financial incentives (i.e. tax holidays, cheap land) played a pivotal role in attracting inward foreign direct investment that had eventually enhanced Korea's competitiveness (Jeong and Pek, 2016). The Masan Export Processing Zone (later renamed as Masan Free Trade Zone) was the first designated bonded processing zone. Consequently, many prominent multinational corporations, such as Nokia, Sony, Sanyo and Matsushita, set up businesses within the zone. This trend not only formed a concentrated cluster that synergized the development of support businesses by Korean companies, it also facilitated the transfer of advanced technologies and business know-how that would later feed the competitiveness and growth of Korean businesses.

Driving a high-technology image

While the 1970s saw Korea relying on heavy industries as the growth engine of its economy, the 1980s initiated seismic shifts towards high-technology products. The shift may have been due in part to the fact that Korea was finding itself sandwiched between its two neighbouring countries, China and Japan. The emergence of China had changed the landscape for trade in Asia, if not the whole world. As China grew on the back of the government's strategy to boost its key heavy and chemical industries, especially in the steel, petrochemical and construction industries, China was fast closing the gap with, if not already overtaken, Korea as the Asian heavy industrial powerhouse. Concurrently, Korea continued to lag behind Japan in high technology innovation and manufacturing.

However, Korean technology products in those early days were still stigmatized by the nation's heavy-industry image. At the start of the high-technology evolution, Korean companies mostly functioned as low-cost assembly lines for foreign consumer electronic firms. By the 1990s, Korea's continued emphasis on high-technology had helped the country move up the value chain to include high-technology sectors such as aerospace and micro engineering. According to a report by Deloitte (GMCI, 2016), Korea had become the global leader in terms of market share for LCD (Liquid Crystal Display) televisions and memory chips, and second to China in the manufacture of smartphones. Overall, in 2014, high technology exports comprised 58 per cent of total manufactured exports.

Korea's rapid ascent in the world of high-technology products is no less due to the government's emphasis on research and development. Currently Korea, along with Israel, is leading the world in being the most research-intensive economy. By 2014, it had spent 4.29 per cent of its GDP on research, and had overtaken the likes of China, the US and the EU (van Nooden, 2016). This amount is twice the global average of 2.23 per cent reported by The World Bank (2015b).

Korea's nation brand image of a high-technology country is also promulgated via its tech-savvy population. The country possesses the world's highest penetration of broadband in households. A recent Forbes report indicated that 99.2 per cent of the 19 million households in Korea have broadband internet access (Ramirez, 2017). Moreover, 99 per cent of household users went online at least once a week and spent an average of 14.3 hours per week on the internet. Given the world dominance of the smartphone market by Samsung and LG, it is also not surprising that mobile phones and smart devices are the most popular means of accessing the internet. Similarly, a study by Pew Research Centre (2016) found that Korea has the highest penetration (about 88 per cent) of smartphone users in the world compared to a global median of 43 per cent. The icing on the cake is the recent announcement that Korea has won the race by being the first country to launch commercial fifth generation (5G) mobile services at the 2018 Winter Olympics at PyeongChang (SCMP, 2018).

Euromonitor's proprietary digital index ranks Korea as the most digitally-connected population globally. The population's openness to new technology has resulted in Korea's tech-savvy population becoming early adopters of technology. For example, according to a report by global market analytics firm eMarketer, nearly one-third of its smartphone users will make mobile payments for goods or services at a point of sale in 2018. Mobile payment adoption took off following the launch of mobile payment services such as Samsung Pay and LG Pay in 2015. Korea's world leading digital network also makes the country ideal for e-commerce. Similarly, with regard to luxury goods, online sales in Korea are expected to outpace the industry's overall growth; see www.luxurysociety.com/en/articles/2017/05/south-South Korea-new-market-luxury-brands/

Samsung – a case in point

The success of Korea's transformation to a high-technology economy and the emphasis it puts on research and development is exemplified by the dominance of

Korean smartphone products. In 2017, Samsung and LG combined held over 70 per cent share of the smartphones market in Korea, with Apple a distant third at 24 per cent. According to Statista, on a worldwide basis, Samsung shipped 317 million units in 2017 and dominated with a share of about 22 per cent, followed by Apple at about 15 per cent.

Samsung was already a successful domestic company at the start of Korea's industrialization process. The firm's main activities were insurance, property and low-technology product manufacturing. The year 1969 was Samsung's first foray into foreign markets by teaming up with the Japanese consumer electronics company, Sanyo, to assemble low-cost transistor radios and black and white televisions. This joint venture gave Samsung the opportunity to send its employees to be trained by Sanyo and other companies. Samsung subsequently mastered not only the manufacturing process but also became innovative in manufacturing and product improvements. By 2007, the company had registered 2,725 patents in the US alone and operated 17 research centres around the globe with an annual R&D expenditure of about USD 5.6 billion. In a short span of two decades, and despite the region, particularly Korea, being embroiled in the Asian financial crisis of 1997, Samsung went on to surpass the Japanese electronics giant Sony in brand value (Brandirectory, 2018). Indeed, the company is ranked higher than quintessential US brands such as Microsoft, American Express, McDonald's, Coca Cola and even Facebook. The Samsung Group, which comprises the combined consumer electronics, information technology and mobile communications businesses, is also five times more valuable than the next Korean brand (ranked 79th), Hyundai Motors, and is ranked fourth globally behind Amazon, Apple and Google (Brandirectory, 2018). The dominance or influence of Samsung in Korea, even in government, is so sprawling that Harlan (2012) in a *Washington Post* article referred to Korea as the "Republic of Samsung."

In a *Harvard Business Review* article published in 2011, Khanna, Song and Lee (2011) asserted that Samsung's success is due in part to the company's ability to tap into its traditional low-cost manufacturing base and augment it with innovations to quickly bring to market high-quality, high-margin products. In doing so, it has melded traditional Confucian top-down management philosophy with Western business practices of meritocracy, where pay and promotion are tied to performance rather than by seniority and by length of stay in the company. This hybrid approach to strategic management has guided Samsung through multiple years of record profits in the wake of the Asian financial crisis in the late 1990s. Khanna et al. (2011) reported that Samsung's profit was higher than the five largest Japanese competitors (Sony, Panasonic, Toshiba, Hitachi and Sharp) combined. Such public and international prominence leave little doubt that advanced technology–as in the case of Germany and Japan–is a representative factor of foreigners' perceived image of Korea (Kinsey and Chung, 2013). However, just as the image of a nation may be inextricably tied to the success of its dominant product brand, its fate is similarly affected by the brand's missteps (Cashen, 2017; Jung, Graeff, and Shim, 2011), such as the battery explosion problem with the Samsung Note 7 smartphone and the corruption charges levelled at the company's Vice Chairman, Lee Jae-yong (Harlan, 2012).

Despite the emphasis on the high technology industry, Korea's heavy industry past has persisted to the present day. An analysis of the Fortune 500 companies indicates that a total of 15 Korean companies made the Fortune Global 500 list in 2017, equalling the number of the previous year, and exceeding by three the number in the 2000 list. While Samsung Electronics is ranked 15th on the list and is the highest-ranking Korean company, the next few remaining Korean companies listed are in the heavy, chemical and construction industry, including Hyundai Motor (78th), SK Holdings (95th), Korea Electric Power Corporation (177th), and with LG Electronics (201st) rounding up the top five. It thus seems that Korea has not totally shed its heavy industry image, nor is it in the country's best interest to do so. Indeed, it is not uncommon for nations to excel in different industry sectors and hence possess multiple brand images, although one image may stand out more than the others. For example, as much as France is known as the fashion capital of the world with its line of luxury brands, France is also known for its heavy industry manufacturing (e.g. Renault and Airbus).

It thus seems that Korea's nation brand image, at least at present, is rooted in its industrialization past. It harbours the pedigree of a competitive heavy-industry nation, coupled with the image of a global high-technology powerhouse. However, as the next section highlights, the Korean government also has other ideas in mind as it continues to forge the nation's image.

Innovation and the future shape of Korea's nation brand

As a measure of a nation's 'ability to generate and sustain inclusive wealth without diminishing the future capability of sustaining or increasing current wealth levels', (GSCI 2017: 8) sustainable competitiveness means that

> current wealth levels are not in danger of being reduced or diminished through over-exploitation of resources (i.e. natural and human resources), the lack of innovative edge required to compete in the globalized markets (i.e. education), or the discrimination, marginalization or exploitation of segments of a society.
>
> (GSCI 2017: 8)

Acknowledging that Korea might have reached the limit of a catch-up strategy focused on industrialization alone, President Park Geun-hye announced in 2013 plans to enhance Korea's sustainable competitiveness by reshaping the focus on developing the country's ability to innovate and be creative (Connell, 2014; Wi and Lee, 2014). As the new growth engine, the 'creative economy' agenda aims to make Korea a global leader in developing innovative products, services and business models in order to continue to propel the country's prosperity and overcoming low growth rates. The creation of the Ministry of Science, ICT and Future Planning (MSIP) and the establishments of Centres for Creative Economy and Innovation across Korea have been instrumental in the development of a creative economy. By 2016, there were 17 such centres across the country and their primary function is to support the growth and overseas expansion of small and medium-sized businesses.

The effort by the government to encourage creativity and innovation is consistent with an article by McKinsey, which suggests that Korea's future lies in high-technology and design rather than in resource-intensive heavy industry (Roach and Lam, 2010). This suggestion is not without merit. As Ollie Wästberg (2009) of the Swedish Institute wrote in *Public Diplomacy Magazine*, IKEA which is well-known for its design is doing more for the image of Sweden than all governmental efforts combined. Thankfully, Korea appears indeed to be heading down this path. In the latest ranking according to the prestigious *iF World Design Guide*, Samsung and LG came in first and third respectively, outranking iconic brands like Hewlett-Packard, Apple, Sony, Miele and BMW. As excellence in product design and quality can enhance a nation brand, Korea needs to do more to capitalize on its emerging stature as global design powerhouse.

Given the recency of President Park's economic policy on creativity and innovation, it is difficult to causally link any policy outcomes to improvements in Korea's sustainable competitiveness. However, if the rankings of the Global Sustainable Competitive Index (GSCI) is anything to go by, it does seem that Korea is on the right path. In the 2015 release of the five-dimensional GSCI, a ranking of 180 globalized economies based on their ability to generate and sustain wealth and dignifying standard of living for their citizens, Korea was ranked fortieth (Furlong, 2015). Among the Asian nations, Korea lagged behind Japan (11th), China (25th) and Singapore (34th). By 2017, Korea (16th) had leapfrogged Japan (20th), China (32nd) and Singapore (54th) (GSCI, 2017).

However, Korea's stellar performance in this index is not evenly reflected in the underlying factors of the index. GSCI (2017) measures overall sustainable competitiveness of a nation based on five pillars of equal importance:

- *Natural Capital*: the given natural environment, including the availability of resources and the level of the depletion of those resources
- *Social Capital*: health, security, freedom, equality and life satisfaction within a country
- *Resource Management*: the efficiency of using available resources as a measurement of operational competitiveness in a resource-constrained world
- *Intellectual Capital*: the capability to generate wealth and jobs through innovation and value-added industries in the globalized markets
- *Governance Efficiency*: Results of core state areas and investments: infrastructure, market and employment structure, the provision of a framework for sustained and sustainable wealth generation.

The report indicates that Korea is ranked 1st globally in intellectual capital and 17th globally in governance efficiency. These outcomes closely align with the current 'creative economy' directions. Korea also ranks 8th in social capital. However, it ranks 148th and 157th respectively in natural capital and resource management. These outcomes, however, are also not surprising given that Korea, like Japan, has not been endowed with abundant natural resources. Indeed, these outcomes lend credence to President Park's initiatives that the best path forward for the country is to capitalize on its people's intellectual capability, through creativity and innovation, to propel growth. In MSIP's own words:

> Creative Economy is to create new markets and jobs by the convergence of science and technology with industry, and the fusion of culture with industry based on the blossoming people's creativity.
>
> (MSIP, 2016)

From a nation brand perspective, it remains to be seen whether Korea will eventually earn a favourably strong image of creativity and innovation, and if so, how long it would take. Some have suggested that while Korea's economic miracle is presently created by giant enterprises that churn out products ranging from ships, buildings and cars, to appliances, electronics goods and semiconductor chips, the continued growth in income and living standards can only come from developing a competitive service sector (Dobbs and Vilinger, 2010). However, evolutionary changes in nation brand image take time. Korea's industrialization process, not unlike the Industrial Revolution in the eighteenth century, is typical of a country that started from unsophisticated low-technology products (i.e. textile and small tools) and then moved up the value chain from there. In this regard, a comparison can be made with the industrialization journey of the US, where cotton farming and the textile industry formed a critical component of the country's economic backbone up until World War II (1939–1945). Another case in point is Britain – once an industrial giant and bastion of the steel industry, this industry has long been in decline together with Britain's image as a heavy-industry nation. Just as Britain has successfully evolved to be regarded highly in innovation and creativity, for example, see the latest Anholt GfK Nations Brand Index (2017),[1] it is left to be seen whether Korea has the soft capabilities of skill, knowledge and resources to eventually transform itself in the same way.

In the first two chapters of Part II, we discussed the formation of Korea's nation brand image and how it evolved with the country's industrialization process. As Korea looks beyond the present decade, the country will continue to face headwinds in enacting a favourable nation brand image as it faces increasing global competition. Along the way, it must also tackle structural issues that impede its nation brand growth. In the next two chapters, we will explore Korea's nation brand at a micro-level by highlighting how Korea's nation brand aids the development of some of Korea's products, particularly those outside the high-technology sector. We will also study the behaviour of Korean consumers by relating their consumption behaviour to their nationalistic dispositions.

Note

1 Britain was ranked 4th for 'creative, cutting edge ideas and new ways of thinking' and 5th for 'major contribution to innovation in science and technology'.

6 Korea's nation brand and its products and consumers

When one thinks of Korean products, the likes of Samsung smartphones, LG televisions and Hyundai cars would probably come to mind. Supported by worldwide advertising and sponsorships of high-profile events,[1] these brands have become household names across the globe. Nevertheless, it is also undeniable that these products are riding on the back of a favourable nation brand image that is congruent with these products. The high-technology nation brand image of Korea signals the quality of Korean electronic products, as much as its innovative heavy-industry image casts a favourable halo on Korean cars.

The branding and image of a nation, and the successful transference of this image to its exports is analogous to the concept of country-of-origin effects. Country-of-origin is a key dimension of nation brand (Dinnie, 2016). It is well-known that nation brand image, through its country-of-origin dimension, has significant impact on the symbolic value of a nation's products, thereby leading companies to leverage or emphasize these distinctive characteristics (Diamantopoulos, Arslanagic-Kalajdzic and Moschik, 2018; Pharr, 2005; Spielmann, 2016; Srinivisan and Jain, 2003; Verlegh and Steenkamp, 1999). When consumers lack objective knowledge about a product or are unable to ascertain a product's true characteristics, they often fall back on their perceptions of the product's country-of-origin to generate stereotypical beliefs about the product (Elliot and Papadopoulos, 2016; C. M. Han, 1989; Lee, Lockshin and Greenacre, 2016). Consequently, consumers favour products from countries with positive images that are congruent to the products, such as Germany and high-technology products or France and fashion products.

It is for the same reason that Audi chooses to emphasize its German heritage, a country synonymous with advanced technology, by adhering to its German slogan *Vorsprung durch Technik* even when marketing in non-German speaking countries, rather than its English or equivalent translation of *Advancement through Technology*. Similarly, Leclerc, Schmitt and Dubé (1994) showed that French-sounding brand names improved the value attributed to hedonic products such as perfume but lowered the perceived value of utilitarian products such as computers. This perception that France is better at manufacturing hedonic than utilitarian products persisted even after consumers had actually experienced the products. Halo effects are thus powerful and well-known in marketing. The power of a nation brand in engendering product perceptions is further demonstrated in an experiment by Liu and Johnson (2005), who showed that even when people had sufficient information to evaluate the product objectively, they still relied on a country image to guide their evaluation.

Just as a positive nation brand image can have positive flow-on effects on a country's products, negative images can be formidable barriers to marketers even if the perceptions are misguided or erroneous (Chattalas, Kramer and Takada, 2008; Johansson, Ronkainen and Czinkota, 1994). Choi and Kim (2014) lamented that while some Korean products have enjoyed a high reputation, other export products are under-priced because their low brand valuations are tied to Korea's nation brand, a phenomenon commonly called the 'Korean Discount' (i.e. undervaluing goods and services of Korean origin). For these products, Korean brands have been criticized as being "stuck in the middle", trapped between an advanced Japan and a cost-competitive China (Roach and Lam, 2010). The Korean Association for Policy Studies (in Choi and Kim, 2014) stated five reasons for the undervaluation of Korean brands: (1) Korea's contribution to international causes which was low compared to its GDP; (2) the Korean people's lack of global citizenship and social etiquette; (3) barriers due to language; (4) a relatively closed society with strong prejudice and discrimination against foreign migrant workers and transnational marriages; and (5) low external awareness compared with Japan and China.

Thankfully, the Korean Discount phenomenon is limited to some product categories, such as textile and mechanical products, to some extent a legacy of the nation's industrial past. On the other hand, products such as consumer electronics, semiconductors and even cars, are enjoying high international reputation. Another category that sees Korean brands enjoying increasing popularity is the area of Korean beauty and fashion products. As the next section discusses, this success has been attributed to the influence of Korea's pop culture or *Hanryu* (한류).

Hanryu (한류) and Korea's beauty and fashion products

Purportedly coined by the media to describe the rapid diffusion of Korean entertainment and culture, the *Hanryu* (한류) neologism of K-pop, K-drama and K-beauty, or generally termed the 'Korean Wave', has swept through the world, first within the Asia Pacific region, and then later into the Middle East, the US, Europe and even South America (Berg, 2018; Cha and Kim, 2011; Cho, 2012; Lee, 2013; Ryoo, 2009). It is beyond the scope of this book to debate why the Korean Wave has garnered such popularity within a short period of time. Suffice to say that some observers believe that mass acceptance of the Korean Wave may be due to the ability of the Korean culture to bridge between Western and Asian values and cultures (Hogarth, 2013; Ryoo, 2009), or to the 'glocalization' of Korean popular culture as referred to by Cha and Kim (2011). Importantly, the successful exports of K-dramas and K-pop music are consistent with the government's economic policy of developing a creative economy that capitalizes on the fusion of culture with industry (MSIP, 2016). In other words, the Korean government is keen to support the development of this entertainment industry because it sees the creation of a favourable image of Korean culture as a source of soft power for public or political diplomacy.

Riding on the back of the success achieved by the Korean Wave, marketing to Korean consumers is rather unique in the world since marketing campaigns disproportionally feature Korean celebrities compared with anywhere else in the world. The consulting and communications agency Millward Brown reported that more than 40 per cent of television advertisements in Korea feature celebrities (Brown, 2014). Moreover, over 85 per cent of these advertisements feature local rather than foreign celebrities. This figure contrasts with celebrity content in China and the USA of about 65 per cent and 50 per cent respectively. These statistics further support the commercial power of *Hanryu* within Korea.

A clear winner that has successfully ridden the *Hanryu* wave is the sector of beauty and skin care products, although the commercial appeal of *Hanryu*-related endorsements is not limited to only these products.[2] Possibly inspired by the handsome male personalities in K-drama and K-pop, Korean men are increasingly conscious of their image.[3] This has propelled Korea to become one of the world's largest markets for men's beauty products. In 2012, sales of skin care products in Korea amounted to USD 565 million or 21 per cent of global sales (International, 2013). Korean men indicate the highest per capita expenditure on skin care products, more than double the next largest market, Denmark.

K-beauty, as the Korean beauty products business sector is commonly called, is not confined to men. Similar to their male counterparts, female Korean celebrities are also influential in the rise of Korean brands overseas. For example, sales of the Korean cosmetic brand *Laneige* in China – K-beauty's largest export market – skyrocketed after its brand ambassador, Song Hye Kyo, starred in the massively popular K-drama *Descendants of the Sun*. However, the success of K-beauty brands should not be linked merely to celebrity endorsements. K-beauty imports into China, its biggest market outside Korea, has come at a time where a gap exists for quality products at a low to mid-range price. K-beauty brands are not considered premium. Their collective image is one of reliable quality at an attractive price. This positioning and pricing of K-beauty products mimic the early days of Samsung, when its brands of consumer electronic products were considered inferior to its Japanese competitors. However, Samsung's brand value has since jumped ahead of Sony's, the quintessential Japanese consumer electronics brand. Just as Samsung's rise coincided with Korea's nation brand image of a superior high-technology nation, K-beauty brands including the likes of SK-II, Etude House, Innisfree and Langeige, have had to be content with playing in the mid-range market, a position that is consistent with Korea's image as a manufacturer of beauty products.

Less is known outside the country regarding Korea's fashion brands; but Korean designers have high aspirations for their creations. The fashion editor of *InStyle Korea*, Sujin Yang, was cited as saying "Spain has Zara, Korea has 8seconds" (http://edition.cnn.com/travel/article/top-South Korean-designers/index.html). The brand was launched in February in 2012 by Samsung subsidiary Cheil Industries to compete against foreign fashion brands such as Spain's Zara, Sweden's H&M and Japan's Uniqlo. A Credit Suisse research report (Suisse 2015) recorded 8seconds sales at USD 54 million in its maiden year, surging to USD 186 million in 2014. The report also stated that 8seconds has targeted sales to reach USD

930 million by 2020. To help in this quest, the company had opened its first overseas store in 2016 in Shanghai China in collaboration with K-pop icon, G-Dragon. Joining forces with *Hanryu* celebrities is hardly surprising.

Despite their success in the domestic market, 8seconds and a range of other Korean streetwear brands, such as MIXXO and Lucky Chouette, are not in the same league as the better-known international labels. Zara, for example achieved global sales in 2016 of USD 17.2 billion, with operations across more than 2,200 stores in 93 countries. Hence, it remains to be seen whether Korean fashion brands, like its K-beauty counterparts, are poised to challenge established international competitors in near future.

In this regard, the relationship between Korea's nation brand image and the performance of Korean brands across all sectors is not unlike those experienced by other countries. It is common for a country to be well-established in one industry or at best in a few limited industries that are highly congruent with the country's brand image, and simultaneously for the country to perform well in certain other sectors with which the country is not generally associated. For example, France dominates the fashion industry with its high-end labels and perfumes such as Louis Vuitton and Chanel and is recognized for its alcohol industry (among others, the Champagne and Bordeaux region products). Some French financial institutions are also among the largest in the world (e.g. the insurance group AXA and BNP Paribas), although one would not typically conjure an image of France as a financial hub or powerhouse. Against a nation brand image of high-technology and heavy industry, the commercial offspring of the Korean Wave (drama, music, beauty and fashion products) are to Korea what AXA and BNP Paribas are to France. It thus remains to be seen whether the Korean Wave phenomenon will help germinate an image of Korea as a creative nation, and in the process possibly dilute its prevailing high-technology, heavy industry image.

The lagging service industries

To further illustrate the congruence, or the lack of it, of Korea's nation brand image with its industries, we shall now discuss Korea's service industry. Globally as well as within the country, the top Korean brands are still dominated by manufacturers. The largest service brand is Korea's mobile telecommunications company, SK Telecom, with a brand value in 2017 of USD 5.23 billion, followed by Shinhan Financial Group with brand value of USD 3.99 billion in 2017 (Brandirectory, 2017). Nevertheless, these two brands pale in comparison to the top Korean brand, the Samsung Group. The two Korean service firms are also far behind global competitors in their respective sectors. For example, in brand value terms, the neighbouring China Mobile is worth USD 46.73 billion, while China's ICBC Bank is worth USD 59.19 billion (Brandirectory, 2018).

A globally vibrant and competitive service sector is crucial to sustain growth and reduce the reliance on the manufacturing sector to almost single-handedly prop up the economy. However, contrasting against the stellar performance of Korea's manufacturing sector, it is apparent that the country's service sector is a gross underperformer. Considering that the country is a developed economy with high per capita income, this lacklustre performance by the service sector as a growth engine is of concern. As Dobbs and Vilinger (2010) put it, Korea must embrace the inevitable fact that its future prosperity will depend less on producing physical things and more on intangibles such as skills, knowledge and information.

While economic nationalistic policies have helped manufacturers attained global stature, the Korean government's efforts to spur on the service sector are not bringing the desired results as quickly as it wishes. A 2012 report by Asian Development Bank identified that a key factor that underpinned this poor performance is government regulations and restrictions (Park, Onghyun and Shin, 2012). The report raised the issue that in the process of protecting the more fragile SME service sector and its jobs through regulations and restrictions, the Korean government may risk stifling the sector's growth and dynamism as these policy measures are likely to be of an anti-competition nature in general. As recently as 2009, the Korean service sector's productivity was the second lowest among OECD economies with Poland taking the bottom spot (Cho, 2009). This is particularly pertinent as Korea already faces and will increasingly face, intense competition from both developed and less developed economies (Thanh and Ji, 2013).

Ironically, the lagging service sector relative to the manufacturing sector is a legacy of the historical and nationalistic push to propel growth led by an export-oriented economy. These actions starve the service sector of investments and resources to build globally competitive brands. Until the early 2000s, Korean banks were prohibited from lending to consumer-service businesses, such as those in tourism and real estate, and were instead encouraged to lend to manufacturing firms. The banking sector is also tightly controlled, with K-Bank and Kakao Bank being the only two banks to be granted retail licences since 1992 (Unit, 2017). It is to be noted that these are internet-based banks. Resonating with this view, a recent article by the BusinessKorea (2014) website has cited regulatory restrictions as the key obstacle to expansion in the service sector, with the service sector facing ten times more restrictions compared to the manufacturing sector.

However, this dismay picture of Korea's service industries belies the effort and investment that the government has put into the industries. Korea appears to be taking steps in the right direction. As the two graphs below illustrate, the contribution of the service sector to overall GDP has been on the rise since the 1990s, although it has somewhat plateaued in the present decade (annual growth for 2017 was about 52.8 per cent). Annual growth in the contribution of the service sector to overall GDP has hovered around 2–3 per cent for the last decade, after having ranged between 4 per cent and 10 per cent in the previous three decades (except for 1997 when the Asian financial crisis saw negative growth of more than 4 per cent).[4] Similarly, the service sector has remained the largest employer, far outstripping those of manufacturing and agriculture. The percentage of people employed in the service sector has grown from under 66 per cent in 2006 to 70.21 per cent in 2016, a figure that is comparable to neighbouring Japan's 70.67 per cent and way ahead of China's 43.5 per cent (Statistica, 2018).

Figure 6.1 Service sector contribution (% of GDP) in Korea
Source: The World Bank (2016b)

The continued liberalization of the service sector appears promising. Immediately following the global financial crisis in 2008–2009, the Ministry of Trade, Industry and Energy reported that capital inflows quickly rose to USD 16.3 billion by 2012 and exceeded USD 21.3 billion in 2016, a record high for capital inflow. The service sector absorbed about 72 per cent or about USD 15.2 billion of this capital inflow, up by 5.3 per cent from 2015. Conversely, investments in the manufacturing sector shrank to USD 5.1 billion, although this figure is still up 12.4 per cent from 2015. The service subsectors that benefitted most from the increased capital inflow are those in information technology, automotive parts and

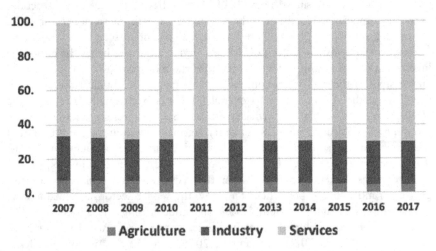

Figure 6.2 Distribution of employment by economic sectors in Korea
Source: Statistica (2017)

logistics. To further aid the development of key service sectors, the Ministry of Strategy and Finance (MOSF) has opened special economic zones (SEZ) that offer incentives to stimulate advanced technology transfer and investment in high-technology services (Jeong and Pek, 2016).

Despite the importance of the service sector to Korea's overall economy–as it would be for any developed economy–it is evident that the present climate in the Korean service sector is more in favour of servicing the domestic market than aspiring to become a global powerhouse. Currently, the insulated Korean financial institutions, among other service institutions, are relatively unknown outside the country. Similarly, while the aging population, coupled with growing levels of income inequality, points to increased demand for financial services for the aged care sector (Park, Onghyun and Shin, 2012), relying on domestic growth will further disincentivize Korean banks from international expansion. Without bringing to public notice the international repute of Korean service companies, the country is unlikely to develop a strong national brand image as a service industry dynamo. As a recent article in EuroMoney (Wilson, 2018) mentions:

> LG and Samsung in electronics, Kia and Hyundai in automobiles, Posco in steel. If this quintet of corporate heavies hailed from Beijing or Tokyo, they would be shadowed constantly by the likes of Industrial and Commercial Bank of China and Bank of Tokyo-Mitsubishi UFJ. But try to remember the last time you heard these lenders mentioned in the global financial media: KEB Hana Bank, KB Kookmin Bank, Shinhan Bank, Woori Bank. They crop up here and there, but usually only when a Korean firm is looking to sell a business unit or fill the books on a juicy IPO or syndicated loan. None is a pan-Asian brand, let alone a known presence on the global stage.

The reverse influence of products on nation brand

Traditionally, research has established that a country's image can be used to promote beliefs about the country's products. For example, consumer perceptions that Germany is superior in high-technology would lead them to surmise that German products are of high quality (Dinnie, 2016; Pharr, 2005; Spielmann, 2016; Srinivisan and Jain, 2003; Verlegh and Steenkamp, 1999). This country-of-origin effect is particularly pertinent when consumers lack objective knowledge about a product or are unable to ascertain a product's true characteristics, and thus rely on the country image as a halo to form stereotypical beliefs about the product (Elliot and Papadopoulos, 2016; C. M. Han, 1989; Lee, Lockshin and Greenacre, 2016).

However, pervasive trade globalization means that consumers are often exposed to foreign products available in their domestic markets. For example, Samsung is a market leader in smartphones and televisions, among other electronics goods, in many countries, and hence many people in the countries to which Samsung exports would have heard of the brand, if not own one or more of its products. In contrast, few have actually visited Korea. For example, Korea Tourist Organization (KTO, 2017) statistics show that inbound American tourists only amounted to about 456,000 in 2017, or about 0.3 per cent of total inbound visitors. Similarly, Japan, Korea's top inbound country, sent close to a million visitors to Korea, a mere 0.7 per cent of total inbound visitors. The same would apply for virtually every country in which Samsung or other Korean brands are present. This finding suggests that consumers are likely to be more knowledgeable about Korea's products than with the country itself.

Consequently, a reverse effect may occur whereby consumers use their beliefs of Korea's products to form perceptions of the country. The logic is as follows: early research suggests that the halo effect works because people have "a fundamental inability to resist the affective influence of global evaluation on evaluation of specific attributes" (Nisbett and Wilson, 1977: 255). The halo effect may be triggered by a related mental stimulus, especially when consumers are unaware that the stimulus may influence their perceptions or behaviour (Bargh, 2002; Fitzsimons et al., 2002). This means that consumers may inadvertently rely on their perceptions of a product (e.g. Samsung televisions are technologically advanced) to form opinions of the country of origin (therefore Korea must be a high-technology country), especially when they do not have direct experience with or knowledge of the country.

Indeed, early psychology experiments had already established the phenomenon of a non-conscious halo by showing that merely exposing people repeatedly to an object could influence their attitude towards the object, especially when conscious processing was minimal or even absent (Bornstein and D'Agostino, 1992; Zajonc, 1968). Similarly, Kleppe, Iversen and Stensaker (2002) posit that some strong brands (e.g. Levi or Mercedes Benz) may be imbued with such strong national identities that they can influence perceptions of the country as well as other unrelated brands from the country. Kleppe et al. (2002) concluded that certain advertising dimensions about a country's products, such as their quality, might unintentionally boost the country's image.

The postulation that the perceptions of a product are capable of shaping the perceptions of the product's country of origin is convincingly shown in a study by Lee and Lockshin (2012). In the study, students from an Australian university were randomly assigned to one of two experimental groups. The context of the experiments were Chile and Chilean copper products. One group was asked to read an article that positioned Chile as a world-class producer of copper artefacts of high quality and exquisite craftsmanship, whereas the second group was exposed to an article the lamented the poor quality and craftsmanship of Chilean copper artefacts. The findings suggest that students who rated the products more positively also possessed more favourable perceptions of Chile and greater intentions to visit the country. A second experiment in the study followed on to show that people would use beliefs about a product to form impressions of a country only when they were unfamiliar with the country.

This reverse-influence effect (from product perceptions to country perceptions) holds significant implications for Korea's nation brand. As we explained earlier, people in most countries where Korean imports are found would then draw on their experience and perceptions of the products to engender images of Korea even though they have not physically been to the country. This means that not only are foreign products competing with each other for domestic customers, but foreign countries are also competing through their products for better images of the country. Since Korea's exports intended for mass consumers are mostly in the technology sector, people are naturally inclined to think of Korea as a high-technology country. While this nation brand image is good news for technology products, it does not augur well for other products. As Choi and Kim (2014) lamented, non-technology exports become less competitive as they suffer from the commonly called phenomenon of the Korean Discount (i.e. undervaluing goods and services of Korean origin). The synergy between Korea's products and its nation brand image means that the government and private industries need to come together on a common country-brand platform. As Mossberg and Kleppe (2005) suggest, programmes that promote nation brand and promotion programmes for the country's export products should be coordinated in order to maximize any synergistic crossover effects.

Consistent with this suggestion, an obvious area that the Korean government has been actively pursuing is promoting the country through *Hanryu*, particularly for the benefit of the tourism sector (Bae, Chang, Park and Kim, 2017; Han and Lee, 2008). Traditionally, Korea is not regarded as a major tourist destination in Asia for various social and political reasons, including the ongoing tensions between North and South Korea (Kim, Long and Robinson, 2009; Kim and Nam, 2016). However, since the year 2000, the *Hanryu* phenomenon has become a catalyst to significant growth in inbound tourist arrivals into Korea. For example, Bae et al. (2017) reported that the number of Japanese tourists to Korea in 2004 jumped by 35 per cent compared to the previous year after the hugely successful K-drama *Winter Sonata* was aired in Japan. Similarly, a KTO survey in 2004 found that 47 per cent of the respondents answered that they were inspired by K-drama to visit Korea (cited in Bae et al., 2017). Similarly, the combination of Korean chicken and beer became popular following the release of *My Love from the Star* (별에서 온 그대), a romantic fantasy about a famous actress and her alien boyfriend (Reuters, 2016).

Indeed, the effects of films on tourism are not new or confined to Korea, for example the movie franchise *The Lord of the Rings* series and its effect on tourism to New Zealand (Croy, 2010; Jones and Smith, 2005). The difference, however, lies in whether and how the country's administration makes concerted efforts to capitalize on the phenomenon to promote the overall brand image of the country for policy and political reasons, beyond the economic gains to particular industry sectors such as entertainment and tourism.

Nationalism and Korean consumers

As economies emerge, a key characteristic in their industrialization process is that their rapid economic growth is fuelled by nationalistic policies that dictate the economic agenda. Economic nationalism, first theorized by the German economist Friedrich List in 1841, encapsulates this perspective as 'a set of policies that results from a shared national identity, and it involves the implementation of economic policy that follows the national purpose and direction, prioritizing national interests above private property and profit motives' (Helleiner, 2002: 310). By directly intervening in the domestic economy, economic nationalistic states enact industrial and trade policies with the aim of protecting domestic firms, particularly those in the early growth stage, from foreign competition. Consequently, these policies, such as import tariffs on foreign goods and restriction on foreign ownership and investments, lead to increased public ownership of enterprises and creation of jobs for nationals. Levi-Faur (1997) described economic nationalism as a triangulation of three interdependent factors: (1) a nation's citizenry sharing a common economic fate, (2) the state playing a crucial and positive role in economic management, and (3) the imperatives of nationalism dictating economic policies to benefit the state. Within the Asia Pacific region, notable examples of successful economic nationalism that propels a nation's economic growth include Japan (Hall, 2004), Taiwan (Wade, 1988), India (D'Costa, 2009) and Korea (Lopez-Aymes, 2010).

Deferring from the traditional definition of economic nationalism, where the state is the consummate actor who sets policies to promote economic progress, economic nationalism at an individual level relates to how the consumption behaviour of individual citizens is underpinned by their desire to help their country, while simultaneously not compromising their self-interest (Akhter, 2007; Baughn and Yaprak, 1996; Lee, Lee and Lee, 2014). Economic nationalistic consumers' preference for domestic products is accompanied by their belief that all parties – citizens, government and domestic firms – have a role to play in reducing the dominance of foreign firms over domestic ones.

Likewise, Korea's nationalism is best described as a co-creation that combines national allegiance and economic self-interest. Patriotic citizens want to support local Korean products, while ensuring that their action would also bring economic benefits to the nation and to themselves (Herald, 2012; Lee, Lee and Lee, 2014). For example, a survey in Korea immediately following the 1997 Asian financial crisis revealed that 78 per cent of respondents professed that they would purchase only Korean products in order to help the country overcome the crisis (cited in Park, Jang and Lee, 2007). Particularly in difficult economic times, people may fear that, left solely to the vagaries of market forces, foreign competition would increase unemployment and widen income inequity. Similarly, in Baughn and Yaprak's (1996) original conceptualization of economic nationalism, the concept reflects the anxiety that arises from the potential inability to control one's economic future in the face of diminished job security. This would then prompt citizens to base their consumption decisions on protecting national economic interests because doing so will ultimately protect their economic interest.

In this sense, economic nationalism is similar to ethnocentrism in that both concepts concern nationalistic feelings that are manifested as a bias in favour of local ones against foreign products. Like economic nationalism, ethnocentrism concerns the proclivity for people to become attached to, or even morally obligated to prefer, things from their own country or culture (LeVine and Campbell, 1972; Shimp and Sharma, 1987). However, a fundamental difference between the two concepts is that economic nationalism contends that the economic prosperity of its citizens rests on first safeguarding the nation's economic well-being (Baughn and Yaprak, 1996; Heilperin, 1960). Hence, the government should purposely and readily support domestic firms because threats from foreign firms would hurt a country's economic well-being and eventually the personal economic security of the citizens.

Interestingly, an outcome of economic nationalism, instigated by the fostering of a common identity among nationals, is the susceptibility to influence from in-group members. In turn, this drives the desire to enhance one's image by choosing products that are perceived as socially or morally acceptable to the in-group members (Lee, Lee and Lee, 2014; Lee, Klobas, Tezinde and Murphy, 2010). Lee et al. (2010) further found that social influence is particularly strong when a brand carries the nation's identity (e.g. Korean Air and British Paints). The results of their study showed that African consumers in a former European colony who had abandoned the national brand in favour of a European brand, were concerned about how fellow nationals would perceive them.

Regardless of the similarities or differences between economic nationalism and ethnocentrism, the two concepts share a common ground based on people invoking a collective identity that is rooted in their country or culture. In her book, *Measured Excess: Status, Gender, and Consumer Nationalism in Korea*, L. C. Nelson (2000) links Korean consumers' purchase decisions to the country's cultural identity and future in an era of economic expansion. She argued that consumer nationalism should go beyond merely avoiding foreign imports and should make choices that are in the best interests of the nation by protecting the nation's cultural honour and preserving its heritage. When domestic alternatives are unavailable, the strong cultural identity means that people would still prefer products from culturally similar countries to those from culturally dissimilar countries (Watson and Wright, 2000). In other words, products can symbolize culture and hence the consumption behaviour of a nation's citizenry both shapes and is shaped by the country's image.

The link between a citizenry's consumption behaviour and the nation's cultural image is particularly pertinent in a collectivistic society like Korea. In such societies, the basis of consumer product choices is often germane to upholding a sense of common cultural identity, accompanied by feelings of belonging among in-groups (nationals) and bias against out-groups (foreigners) (El Banna, Papadopoulos, Murphy, Rod and Rojas-Méndez, 2018; Johnson, 1965; Lau and Lee, 2018; Nelson, 2000).

Ironically, just as economic nationalism has increased the country's wealth and enriched the population, economic growth has also spurred greater consumption of foreign products and adoption of foreign culture, especially those of Western origin (Njau, 2013; Yi, 2002). This trend in turn has led to a rise in cosmopolitanism particularly among the younger generation, who are more inclined to admire and desire things that are associated with a Western lifestyle (Alden, Steenkamp and Batra, 2006; Cleveland, Laroche and Papadopoulos, 2009; Lee, Lee and Lee, 2014). Tracing back to early works by Merton (1957) who distinguishes between two types of influential persons (locals versus cosmopolitans), cosmopolitanism orientates people beyond the confines of their immediate neighbourhood to participate in an expanded society. Cosmopolitanism in a consumer behavioural sense means that people are open to different cultures, or may even actively seek experiences from cultures other than their own (Riefler, Diamantopoulos and Siguaw, 2012; Steenkamp and de Jong, 2010; Yi, 2002).

Consistent with this trend, Korea is following the footsteps of other developed economies. With an estimated per capita gross national income of about USD 36,000 and positioning the country as the 30th richest in the world by gross national income (The World Bank, 2016a), Korean consumers possess relatively high disposable income. With this increasing affluence, their consumption behaviour increasingly mimics that of developed economies by being more brand conscious. Tech-savvy Korean consumers typically research products online and are well-informed when purchasing a product. Consequently, they have become more inclined to purchase non-domestic products, often at much higher prices than domestic equivalents. As they embrace international influences, Korean consumers are willing to pay for well-known brands, as such behaviour reflects the social status of individuals (Kim, Knight and Pelton, 2009; Park, Rabolt and Sook Jeon, 2008).

Inspired by the lifestyles portrayed by the media and youth pop culture, Koreans increasingly view material possessions as a sign of success and place greater emphasis on the conspicuous consumption of products such as fashion items, that reflect certain desired symbolic meanings or values. Consequently, Korean consumers are becoming less concerned with buying products made in Korea. This behaviour is underpinned by the need for value-expressiveness, especially of Western culture and products in the younger generation. Defined as one's psychological need for self-esteem, a sense of belonging or respect (Kelman, 1961; Nelson and McLeod, 2005; Park and Lessig, 1977), a value-expressive identity refers to how people relate to certain identities or social groups, and consequently adopt the behaviours of the identities or groups. Value-expressiveness often relates to people associating with film or pop stars in order to project a self-image, thereby resulting in them adopting the identities' behaviours and preferences. For instance, a study involving 5,586 German adolescents showed that movie stars' smoking behaviour significantly influenced adolescent smoking initiations as well as their continued smoking behaviour (Hanewinkel and Sargent, 2007). According to Moschis and Churchill (1978), young people's social identity may be part of the process of socialization as they develop consumer-related skills, knowledge and attitudes by imitating their peers.

It is likely that the signing of free trade agreements between Korea and various countries have also helped international competitors make inroads into Korea, thereby further fuelling the rise in cosmopolitanism.[5] For example, the 2007 Korea-US Free Trade Agreement (KORUS FTA) has reduced or totally eliminated tariffs for over 90 per cent of US imports. Similarly, agreements with the EU (2010) and Australia (2014) have helped make Korea an attractive market for foreign brands. Just Western fashion, for example, a series of global fashion names, including H&M and 6ixty8ight, have opened stores in Korea since 2010. The second-largest US sportswear company, Under Armour, started operating in Seoul's upmarket Gangnam district in 2016. Yet another simple example to illustrate the adoption of Western culture through product consumption in Korea is the proliferation of international coffee chains, such as the quintessential US label Starbucks, across Korea. The appeal lies in the stores being viewed as a symbol of wealth and international sophistication, especially among the middle class (Kim, 2016). The increasing presence of and easy access to foreign products in the domestic market is no doubt fuelling the rise in cosmopolitanism among Koreans consumers.

The crux of the matter is as follows: against a backdrop of growing cosmopolitanism, conspicuous consumption of foreign goods and adoption of Western lifestyle and culture, how well can Koreans remain attached to their cultural roots and maintain an image that is uniquely Korean? Just as rapid industrialization brings about prosperity to the country, it also erodes, at least partially, traditional values and culture associated with Korea (Hyun, 2001; Yi, 2002).

Despite this outward looking perspective, nationalistic fervour still resonates to some extent among the Korean populace to drive their preference for things that are 'their own' (Lee, Lee and Lee, 2014; Tsai, Yoo and Lee, 2013). The country has come a long way since being viewed as an impoverished nation after the post-Korean War period. The identity of the country and its people, which stemmed from the historical past and projected into the future, has fostered a close link between an individual self and the collective society. As the country and its fortune evolves, so does the perceived image of Korea as a country in the eyes of the locals and as importantly, of the outside world.

Indeed, Korea has a history of limiting or criticizing foreign goods consumption. Starting from the 1980s when such consumption was labelled as unpatriotic by government-led movements, to the period during the 1997 Asian financial crisis when Koreans were urged to buy only Korean products, a strong sense of consumer nationalism prevails to this day. A case in point is the fashion label Zara in Korea: Zara was criticized for the poor or lack of social contributions to the country since its inception in 2011 (Bizwire, 2017), as well as for the criticism levelled by the company's CEO of ordinary Koreans who joined a rally against the scandal-plagued President Park Geun-hye (Park, 2018). However, such isolated incidents are unlikely to succeed against the tide of mass consumerism that has brought about the country's economic progress.

In summary, Korea is traditionally a collectivistic society, starting from when Confucianism was adopted as the ruling ideology of the Choson dynasty (1392–1910). However, rapid globalization through industrialization coupled with indiscriminate permeation of Western culture and goods have led to Korean traditional culture giving way to and becoming tainted with Western culture. This experience of balancing two possibly conflicting identities – traditional versus contemporary – is not uncommon among non-Western developed countries. For example, in their post-modernistic narrations of the experiences of expatriate professionals in Singapore, Thompson and Tambyah (1999) found that in trying to enact a cosmopolitan identity, the expatriates often faced countervailing tensions from having to negotiate between adapting to a cosmopolitan lifestyle on the one hand, and the enduring ties to affiliations and familiar things from their home country on the other. Like other countries, Korea will have to adjust the equilibrium between sustaining its traditional cultural heritage and infusion of Western culture into its seemingly homogenous society.

Notes

1 For example, Samsung is a worldwide sponsor of the Olympic Games, while Kia is a regular sponsor the top-class tennis events like the Australian Open.
2 For example, viewers would be forgiven if they were to guess that a recent TV advertisement featuring the Korean actress Jun Ji Hyun (전지현) was for some form of beauty products rather than *Ottogi* (오뚜기) cup noodles (the advertisement may be viewed at www.youtube.com/watch?v=jqeR0mrodRs). Nonetheless, such marketing communication ploys again show the prevailing reliance on *Hanryu* (한류) endorsements in product marketing.
3 For example, the popular male actor, Lee Min-ho, endorses the beauty product brand, *Innisfree.*
4 Arguably, the slow growth of the service sector may in part be reflecting the difficult structural changes as the country moves from a manufacturing-led economy to a more balanced economy with a greater role for the service sector.
5 The opening of the Korean market has led to some sectors been dominated by foreign brands e.g. pet food (see http://South Koreansafari.com.au/content/pet-food-South Korean-pet-food-market-dominated-foreign-brands).

7 Concluding remarks

In broader terms, this book has deviated from conventional economic and market approaches, which focus on major economic variables (e.g., gross domestic product, inflation, interest and exchange rate, comparative advantages or factor endowments) in the economic growth of Korea. Instead, this study has adopted a broader application of socio-economic, cultural and political change associated with the transition of Korea's growth paradigm from the 1990s to the present period. In doing so, we argue that in addition to scrutinizing macro/micro economic factors (such as exchange realignments, changes of wage levels and trade performance), analyzing the impacts of non-market factors such as government-business and government-society relations in Korea's economic growth since the 1960s can offer further and more profound insights into contemporary Korean political economy. Three key areas of the Korean economy over the last five decades are examined in this book, namely, evolution of the Korean political economy, the competitive transition of the Korean political economy and the maturing economy of Korea particularly from a nation branding perspective.

Evolution of the Korean political economy

The first part of this book was dedicated to enriching the existing knowledge of the evolution of the Korean political economy from the early process of Korea's industrialization (1960s) to the period of Korea's globalization drive by the Kim Dae-jung and Park Geun-hye (1998–2017) regimes. We have also briefly reviewed various theoretical paradigms of Korea's economic growth since the 1960s in order to examine how the evolution of the Korean political economy has been dealt with by scholars historically as well as theoretically. In particular, we looked at the evolution of the dynamics of socio-political and economic changes in Korea since the arrival of the Kim Dae-jung administration (1998) which faced one of the most daunting economic challenges (i.e. the 1997 financial crisis) faced by Korea in the history of the country's industrialization process.[1] We have also examined the changing nature of economic and policy agendas, Korean business culture and business environment from Kim Dae-jung to Park Geun-hye and to the Moon Jae-in regime. We have questioned whether a new growth paradigm has emerged and consequently whether a new Korean market environment in terms of international business, has been created, shaped and sustained by the advent of Korea's entry into the global economy as a capital importer since the early 2000s.

Undoubtedly, as revealed in the discussion in Chapter 2, Korea's experiences of the 1997 Asian financial crisis constituted one of the most critical factors that moved the country away from the centrally planned government-directed investment model, towards a more market-oriented model that led the nation into a new market and business environment. Figures relating to inflow of foreign direct investment (FDI) into the Korean market during the late 1990s and onwards clearly substantiate the new trend. As discussed and argued throughout the first part of this book, it is the way in which domestic factors, such as the exercise of government power, government policies, domestic social classes and political forces, react to the rapidly changing international division of labour that are significant factors in Korea's economic order. This is not to say that the conventional economic and market approaches are deficient. Nevertheless, Korea's rapidly changing market environment should not be treated solely as a consequence of the economic crisis or a political crisis, but as a result of a structural crisis of the Korean political economy accumulated over four decades.

The Korean case clearly shows that structural and institutional factors such as state-capital relationships affected by internal and external factors in the course of capitalist industrialization – all of which have driven a set of different targets for the state in achieving economic and political goals – do not seem to influence Korea's development trajectory. The significant increase of foreign capital in Korea from the late 1990s has been closely related to the Korean state's change in economic policies, particularly towards foreign capital. These economic activities, whether neo-liberal or neo-mercantilist, adopted during the process of capitalist industrialization, have been found to be subordinate to the goal of state building and the interests of the state. This finding suggests a very different consideration from the tradition of economic liberalism, which emphasizes factor endowments. For example, even today in every part of the Korean political economy, the characteristics of an undisputed presidential system are yet to disappear. A key objective of the current Moon administration's (May 2017 to present) reform policies, also known as Moon's J-nomics, is to eliminate the reliance on 'trickle-down economics' instigated by the two former conservative presidents, Lee Myung-bak and Park Geun-hye. President Moon, who was elected on the back of populist pledges to create jobs and reduce inequality in a nation that has for decades been dominated by a handful of wealthy conglomerates (*Chaebol*), believes the government should deregulate the market and help the rich and particularly the *Chaebol* so that their income and wealth can trickle down and increase the general prosperity.

Under J-nomics, most economic policies concerning debt, tax reform, conglomerates and fiscal stimulus, have been overturned with the aim of more equitable growth. The change has been so drastic that pundits are talking about a 'paradigm shift' for the Korean economy from the previous neo-classical model to an income-led growth paradigm. In general, the logic of 'income-led growth' is that if people's wages increase, by the Government for instance, they will have more money at their disposal and will increase their spending. People will buy products from companies, and as such this would make companies invest and hire more people to produce more, ultimately leading to growth. In fact, in January 2018 a drastic minimum wage hike took place. Consequently, from February 2018, a shorter working week (52 hours instead of 68 for companies with more than 300 employees) has taken effect. While some economists believe Moon's J-nomics approach is timely amid rising income inequality, others claim that it could stunt Korea's growth prospects and stifle corporate innovation that would weaken Korea's overall global competitiveness.[2] Thus, this book reveals that each of the Korean regime's growth trajectories is still directed largely by the state-led developmental and neo-mercantilist policies under the presidential system. Thus, all vestiges of the collectivist nature of state-led political economy have yet to disappear.

Korean political economy in transition

With regard to the Korean economy's transition, it is clear that the post-1997 era, which seemingly brought about a fundamental overhaul of the structure of the Korean political economy, contributed to the change of the Korean market image among foreign companies or multinational corporations (MNCs). This book attempted to uncover some previously neglected insights into the Korean market and explored the social and political factors, as well as the way that culture impacts on MNCs and the Korean brand image. A crucial finding from the discussion in Chapter three is that the qualitative in-depth interviews in this study substantiate the view that there is a strong correlation between the Korean government's economic nationalistic policies and the decline of inward FDI in Korea. While it is true that the 1997 financial crisis brought about a different market dynamism and that for the first time in modern Korean capitalism, issues like transparency, accountability and lessened government intervention have been major themes in the local and foreign business community, Chapter 3 of this book substantiates that Korea's strong political and economic culture that has prioritized national interest and security over ideology, is still prevalent in Korean society. While the interview results in this study are based on earlier fieldwork conducted in Korea in 2010, they still seem to be valid in 2018 since the negative images of the Korean market today are often regarded as one of the risk factors that make many MNCs choose other markets over Korea (*The Business Times*, 2018).

According to a recent survey conducted by *The Korea Economic Daily* (*Hankuk Kyungje Sinmun*, 2018), with 40 CEOs of multinational corporations operating in Korea, 42 per cent of the interviewees postponed their decisions to reinvest in Korea due to a labour-management dispute (85 per cent), increase of wage rate (72.5 per cent) and regulations (70 per cent). The data shows that the collective nature of economic nationalism (i.e. market access barriers in the form of regulations/rules against foreign businesses in Korea) mobilized by the state is still perceived as prevalent by the MNCs. Hence, whatever dominant shape Korea's competitiveness will take in the future to be successfully integrated into the global economy, would not only depend on domestic industries and economic, but to what extent and how the country will be able to improve and reshape its current image of being a difficult market for international business. Thus, the country must be open to criticism and establish a realistic and comprehensive strategy, which should aim at transforming the country into a mature economy, with a more open, transparent, competitive, globalized and culturally dynamic society.

A maturing Korea and its nation brand image

As Korea looks to the next decade and enters the stage of a mature economy, the country will continue to grapple with the challenges of maintaining or even improving its nation brand image in the face of increasing competition globally. Building a strong nation brand through culture as a soft power is another path that Korea is actively pursuing. However, while successive administrations have tried to build a strong cultural identity, Korea is disadvantaged in several ways. First, it lacks internationally recognized symbols. For instance, Beijing has the Great Wall, Sydney has the Opera House, and Hong Kong has its harbour and the skyline of skyscrapers. Seoul, let alone other Korean cities, does not possess a symbol that would signify it as a global cultural city. Second, the 2016 population census puts the number of foreigners of non-Korean ethnicity at about 1.4 million or 2.8 per cent of the population (Korea, 2016). Korea also lacks the credentials to be a genuinely global and cosmopolitan country. Third, while the K-wave export of films and music may have successfully portrayed the modernized side of Korea to some Asian countries, it has limitations in helping the nation build its cultural heritage globally.

It does indeed seem that although Korea has climbed the global ranking in terms of nation brand (NBI, 2017), the country is likely to face stronger headwinds than in the past as it attempts to extend its upward trajectory. However, the world in which Korea was situated prior to the twentieth century, when its rapid industrialization had great momentum, is drastically different from the one that it is experiencing today. The international economic order is different, with China and the Asia Pacific region in general driving a shift of the centre of economic gravity towards the East. The political and military landscape is also shifting as reassessments of security threats drive greater defence spending funded by economic growth (Ablett and Erdmann, 2013). To make matter worse, North Korea is perpetuating regional instability. Competitiveness from technology is short-lived due to continual disruptive innovations. Traditional Eastern culture is constantly under the threat of dilution from Western influences. These uncertainties are a confronting challenge as well as an opportunistic prospect for Korea to build on what it has already achieved in terms of its nation brand.

Finally, it is not possible to discuss the shape of Korea's future brand image without considering the potential reconciliation with North Korea. Just as President Kim Dae-jung's Sunshine Policy (officially The Reconciliation and Cooperation Policy *vis-à-vis* the North 햇볕 정책) laid initial theoretical grounds to reunite the two Koreas through economic development, tourism and cultural exchanges, the legacy of the current regime of President Moon Jae-in may indeed be defined by its seemingly soft approach to conciliation, one that appears to have robust public support (Park, 2017). As Korea shifts focus to becoming a creative economy, it is harnessing its industrialization experience to aid North Korea. Following the inter-Korea summit between President Moon Jae-in and North Korean leader Kim Jong Un in April 2018, major conglomerates such as Lotte, Hyundai and Hyosung have announced plans to explore inter-Korean ventures, including resuming operations at the defunct Kaesong joint industrial complex in North Korea, as well as potentially connecting the railways of the two nations. Sport diplomacy, such as the joint flag bearers in the 2018 Winter Olympics at PyeongChang and the joint women's ice hockey team, also represents an effort to strengthen bilateral ties.

As Korea's nation image has been potentially tarnished by external perceptions of its northern neighbour (Schröter and Schwekendiek, 2015), improving the image of North Korea would indirectly help Korea's own image. Whether the improvement of North Korea's image comes as a consequence of reconciling the two Koreas – which would see the South's stature diffusing into the North, in a fashion similar to the reconciliation of the two German states – or simply by the improvement in economic and social conditions in North Korea, the outcome would be positive for Korea. However, it remains to be seen which path the two Koreas will take. If history is anything to go by, the process will be long and unpredictable.

Conclusion

Korea's economic development has been, by any scale, outstanding; currently the fourth largest economy in Asia and eleventh largest in the world. The nation has recorded an average annual economic growth of over 8 per cent during the period between the 1960s and 1990s. In this period, per capita gross national product (GNP) increased from a meagre USD 80 (1960) to USD 10,500 (1999), with real GNP growth since 1960 expanding by an average of 8 per cent per annum (The World Bank, 2015a). Within the next two decades, by 2017, Korea's per capita income nearly topped USD 30,000. As the fifth largest exporter in the world, Korea's trade volume exceeded USD 1 trillion in 2017. These elements have converted the image of Korea from that of a primarily agrarian country and a historical recipient of ODA (official development assistance) up until 1995, to that of a newly industrializing country (NIC) based on manufacturing and services in the 1990s and the twenty-fourth member of the Development Assistance Committee (DAC), the international donor's club.[3] Korea's management, with its support for hard-working, low-cost and disciplined labour, reliance on foreign capital and the creation of bureaucracies and the *Chaebol*, has contributed to Korea's remarkable export performance and *Chaebol*-led capital accumulation.

Like Japan in the 1970s, however, Korea in the 1980s and the 1990s has been confronted by dilemmas caused by its own economic success. These dilemmas included the emergence of new protectionism by advanced industrial countries such as the US, and the EU, and the obvious competition from the newly emerging economic superstars, India and China. At home, there were other challenges.

These included rising social, ideological and political tension, rapidly widening gap between the haves and have-nots, and worsening structural imbalances in the economy, particularly between high-tech/low-tech industries and small and medium-sized firms. The challenges arising from the effort to move towards a more mature economy, have led Korea over the past three decades (1997–2018) to new growth paradigms compared to the country's previous growth trajectory set by the government/*Chaebol*-led 'export-led high-speed industrialization'. This paradigm shift requires the government to design appropriate and consistent policies that promote efficiency, technology and entrepreneurship.

Korea entered the new millennium with a new and critical phase in its industrial and technological development based on the liberalization of the economy through foreign direct investments (FDI). The neo-liberal nature of globalization and the open and expanding market in Korea in the late twentieth century have brought about political, institutional and socio-cultural transformation, along with the shift in Korea's developmental growth paradigm. In fact, one of the most dynamically changed objectives in Korea's economic policy since the collapse of Korean currency during the 1997 financial crisis, has been the resolve to become a major player in the Northeast Asian market through inward foreign direct invest-ment (Northeast Asian business hub) and a regional free trade agreement (FTA) hub aimed at regional economic integration. With this goal set as a policy focus, the Korean government under President Kim Dae-jung and later President Roh Moo-hyun, has sought to make Korea a prime location for foreign investors and has successfully engaged with FTAs to overcome the currency crisis on the one hand, and to strengthen Korea's global competitiveness and continuously boost exports on the other hand. From the early 1990s, the affiliates of over 16,000 foreign multinational corporations (MNCs) have established operations in fields ranging from consumer products to high-tech industries operating in Korea. According to the *World Investment Report 2006* arising from the United Nations Conference on Trade and Development (UNCTAD), the inward FDI stock in Korea as a percentage of current GDP in 2005 was 8.0 per cent, above Japan's 2.2 per cent. Furthermore, Korea has emerged in recent decades as one of the most active states in the world and has pursued FTAs with partners across the globe. Since the first bilateral FTA with Chile in 2004, over the past 14 years (2004–2018), Korea has concluded fifteen FTAs with 52 countries, namely with Chile, Singapore, EFTA (European FTA), ASEAN, India, the EU, Peru and the US, and has recently successfully concluded FTA negotiations with Colombia, Turkey, Australia, New Zealand, Canada, China and Vietnam (Korea FTA Portal, 2018).

This new shift towards a more open and globalized economy is a unique development given one notable characteristic of the country's rapid economic growth, namely, this success would have been unlikely without strong economic nationalism, stimulated initially by a negative response to earlier interactions with foreign regimes, and then by the desperate need for economic survival in the 1970s and 1980s. Though modern Korea has found it imperative to integrate into a global economy, the once successful but overly regulated external policies adopted prior to the financial crisis have become an obstacle to Korea's endeavour to join the more open and competitive global market as a major player. Oscillation between economic nationalism and global openness may not be a phenomenon unique to Korea. This tendency could potentially surface in countries with strong traditional values, driven and led by a strong state in a transitional stage, and planning to shift towards a more mature economy. However, the impressive and positive portrayal of Korea's openness to trade and FDI in the aftermath of the financial crisis should not mislead readers into thinking that Korea's reform measures have proceeded smoothly. On the contrary, painful and difficult decisions must be made, and were made, along the road towards conforming to global standards.

As Korea looks beyond its current position, the country will continue to face the challenges of assuring buoyant economic growth, consumer welfare gains and job creation by expanding trade and investment, as well as maintaining or even improving its nation brand image in the face of increasing competition globally. Furthermore, there are rising threats from a resurgent Japan, Korea's inability to compete with China on a large scale, instability in the South China Seas, and a potential reconciliation with a menacing northern neighbour. Korea wants its international standing to be commensurate with the economic success it has built since the 1960s. Hence, whatever dominant shape Korea's competitiveness and nation brand image will take in the future will depend on the industries that the country is able to develop and sustain competitively during its fourth industrial revolution.

In conclusion, it should be noted that various findings resulting from this study cannot be taken as conclusive. This observation is largely due to data limitations, the rapidly changing socio-economic and political, domestic and international environment on the Korean peninsula arising from geopolitics over North Korean nuclear issues, and the scarcity of prior research on the subject of MNC behaviour and the impact of MNCs on the maturity of the Korean economy. The results of the present study suggest that further research (i.e. current debate over the J-nomics growth strategy) is justified. Nevertheless, we believe that the research conducted here on the evolution and transition of Korea as a mature economy has gone far beyond anything attempted before.

Notes

1 Korea, then the eleventh largest economy in the world, was the hardest hit by the 1997 Asian financial crisis. On 21 November 1997, the Korean government officially requested emergency assistance from the International Monetary Fund (IMF), receiving a USD 58 billion bailout package from the IMF. For the first time in the entire history of Korean industrialization, Korea experienced the worst economic growth in 1998, which consequently marked the end of Korea's long hailed reputation as 'Asian dragon'.

2 Despite President Moon and his team's efforts of J-nomics and income-led growth over the past 18 months (May 2017–November 2018), various economic indicators in late 2018 show unfavourable results of the policy. The Bank of Korea lowered its gross domestic product growth forecast for 2018 from 3 per cent to 2.7 per cent. Unemployment has also been increasing as Korea's stronghold in traditional manufacturing industries, such as shipbuilding and automobiles, shed jobs amid increasing competition from lower cost Chinese rivals. As a consequence, on 10 November 2018, President

Moon replaced chief presidential policy aide Jang Ha-sung and finance minister Kim Dongyeon, the two most senior policymakers in charge of running J-nomics' signature polices (i.e. minimum wage increase/a shorter work week).

3 The DAC is part of Organization for Economic Cooperation and Development (OECD). The key function of the DAC is to promote and contribute to the sustainable global economic growth, poverty eradication and improvement of living standards in developing countries. There are currently 30 members in the DAC (OECD 2018).

References

Ablett, J., and Erdmann, A. (2013). Strategy, scenarios, and the global shift in defense. Retrieved from www.mckinsey.com/industries/public-sector/our-insights/strategy-scenarios-and-the-global-shift-in-defense-power

Ahearne, J. (2009). Cultural policy explicit and implicit: A distinction and some uses. *International Journal of Cultural Policy*, 15(2), 141–153.

Akhter, S. H. (2007). Globalization, expectations model of economic nationalism, and consumer behavior. *Journal of Consumer Marketing*, 24(3), 142–150.

Alden, D. L., Steenkamp, J.-B. E. M., and Batra, R. (2006). Consumer attitudes toward marketplace globalization: Structure, antecedents and consequences. *International Journal of Research in Marketing*, 23(3), 227–239.

Amsden, A. (1987a). *Asia's Next Giant: South Korea and Late Industrialization*. New York: Oxford University Press.

Amsden, A. (1987b). *Republic of Korea – Country Study*. Helsinki: World Institute for Development Economics Research of the United Nations University.

Amsden, A. (1992). A Theory of Government Intervention in Late Industrialization. In L. Putterman and D. Rueschemeyer (eds), *State and Market in Development: Synergy or Rivalry?*: 53–84. Boulder, CO, and London: Lynne Rienner Publishers.

Amsden, A. (1994). Why Isn't the Whole World Experimenting with the East Asian Model to Develop? Review of The East Asian Miracle. *World Development*, 22(4), 627–633.

Analytics, A. (2006). College students clueless about brands' origin. Retrieved from www.marketingcharts.com/industries/telecom-industries-462

Anholt, S. (2005). Nation brand as context and reputation. *Place Branding*, 1(3), 224–228.

Anholt, S. (2006). The Anholt-GMI city brands index: How the world sees the world's cities. *Place Branding*, 2(1), 18–31.

Anholt, S. (2007). *Competitive Identity: The New Brand Management for Nations, Cities and Regions*. New York: Palgrave Macmillan.

Anholt, S. (ed.) (2008). *From Nation Branding to Competitive Identity – The Role of Brand Management as a Component of National Policy*. Oxford: Butterworth-Heinemann.

Bae, E.-S., Chang, M., Park, E.-S., and Kim, D.-C. (2017). The effect of Hallyu on tourism in Korea. *Journal of Open Innovation: Technology, Market, and Complexity*, 3(4), 22.

Bargh, J. A. (2002). Losing Consciousness: Automatic Influences on Consumer Judgment, Behavior, and Motivation. *Journal of Consumer Research*, 29(2), 280–285.

Baughn, C. C., and Yaprak, A. (1996). Economic Nationalism: Conceptual and Empirical Development. *Political Psychology*, 17(4), 759–778.

Berg, S.-H. (2018). Local Buzz, Global Pipelines and Hallyu: The Case of the Film and TV Industry in South Korea. *Journal of Entrepreneurship and Innovation in Emerging Economies*, 4(1), 33–52.

Bizwire, K. (2017). Sales of Zara Soar in South Korea Despite Criticism. Retrieved from http://koreabizwire.com/sales-of-zara-soar-in-south-korea-despite-criticism/84516

Bornstein, R. F., and D'Agostino, P. R. (1992). Stimulus recognition and the mere exposure effect. *Journal of Personality and Social Psychology*, 63(4), 545–552.

Brandirectory (2017). The Most Valuable Brands in 2017. Retrieved from http://brandirectory.com/league_tables/table/global-500-2017

Brandirectory (2018). The World's Most Valuable Brands in 2018. Retrieved from http://brandirectory.com/league_tables/table/global-500-2018

Brown, M. (2014). What Are the Benefits of Celebrity-Based Campaigns? *Perspectives*, 6 (4), 13–16.

Browning, C. S. (2015). Nation branding, national self-esteem, and the constitution of subjectivity in late modernity. *Foreign Policy Analysis*, 11(2), 195–214.

BusinessKorea (2014). Korea's Service Industry Subject to 10X More Red Tape than Manufacturing Industry. Retrieved from www.businesskorea.co.kr/english/news/industry/3201-regulation-service-sector-korea's-service-industry-subject-10x-more-red-tape

Cashen, E. (2017). Samsung survives exploding phones and allegations of bribery to start 2017 strongly. Retrieved from www.theneweconomy.com/business/samsung-survives-exploding-phones-and-allegations-of-bribery-to-start-2017-strongly

Cha, H., and Kim, S. (2011). A Case Study on Korean Wave: Focused on K-POP Concert by Korean Idol Group in Paris, June 2011. *Communications in Computer and Information Science*, 263(Spring), 153–162.

Cha, V. D. (2005). South Korea in 2004: Peninsular Flux. *Asian Survey*, 45(1), 33–40.

Chamberlin, P. F. (2001). *Korea 2010: The Challenges of the New Millennium*. Washington, DC: Centre for Strategic and International Studies.

Chang, H. (1998). South Korea: The Misunderstood Crisis. In K. S. Jomo (ed.), *Tigers in Trouble*: 223–231. London: Zed Books.

Chattalas, M., Kramer, T., and Takada, H. (2008). The impact of national stereotypes on the country of origin effect: A conceptual framework. *International Marketing Review*, 25(1), 54–74.

Chey, H.-K., and Helleiner, E. (2018). Civilisational values and political economy beyond the West: the significance of Korean debates at the time of its economic opening. *Contemporary Politics*, 24(2), 191–209.

Cho, D. (2009). The Republic of Korea's Economy in the Swirl of Global Crisis. Asian Development Bank Institute (ADBI) Working Paper No.147. Tokyo: ADBI.

Cho, Y. (2008). The national crisis and de/reconstructing nationalism in Korea during the IMF intervention. *Inter-Asia Cultural Studies*, 9(1), 82–96.

Cho, Y. Y. (2012). Public Diplomacy and South Korea's Strategies. *Korean Journal of International Studies*, 10(2), 275–296.

Choi, D., and Kim, P. S. (2014). Promoting a policy initiative for nation branding: The case of South Korea. *Journal of Comparative Asian Development*, 13(2), 346–368.

Choi, I. (2011) Korea: a country case analysis. In *BRIE (Berkeley Roundtable on the International Economy), Green growth: from religion to reality—seven case studies on ambitious strategies to shape green growth*. Berkeley: BRIE.

Choi, J. (1993). Political Cleavages in South Korea. In H. Koo (ed.), *State and Society in Contemporary Korea*: 13–50. Ithaca, NY, and London: Cornell University Press.

Chu, Y-H. (1989). State Structure and Economic Adjustment of the East Asian Newly Industrializing Countries. *International Organization*, 43(4), 647–672.

Chung, K. H. (1974). Industrial Progress in South Korea. *Asian Survey*, 14(5), 439–455.

Cleveland, M., Laroche, M., and Papadopoulos, N. (2009). Cosmopolitanism, Consumer Ethnocentrism, and Materialism: An Eight-Country Study of Antecedents and Outcomes. *Journal of International Marketing*, 17(1), 116–146.

Clifford, M. L. (2016). *Troubled Tiger: Businessmen, Bureaucrats and Generals in South Korea*. London: Routledge.

Cole, D. C., and Lyman, P. N. (1971). *Korean Development*. Cambridge, MA: Harvard University Press.

Connell, S. P. (2014). Creating Korea's Future Economy: Innovation, Growth, and Korea-US Economic Relations. *Analysis from East-West Center, 111* (January), 1–8.

Connell, S. (2013). Korea's creative economy agenda. *Asia Pacific Bulletin*, 229, 1–2, September 6.

Corsetti, G., Pesenti, P., and Roubini, N. (1998). Paper Tigers? A Preliminary Assessment of the Asian Crisis. Paper Presented at the Conference on NBER-Bank of Portugal International Seminar on Macroeconomics. Lisbon, 14–15 June.

Crane, G. (1998). Economic nationalism: bringing the nation back in. *Millennium: Journal of International Studies*, 27(1), 55–75.

Crotty, J., and Lee, K. (2001). Economic Performance in Post-Crisis Korea: A Critical Perspective on Neoliberal Restructuring. *Seoul Journal of Economics*, 14(2), 183–242.

Croy, W. G. (2010). Planning for Film Tourism: Active Destination Image Management. *Tourism and Hospitality Planning & Development*, 7(1), 21–30.

D'Costa, A. P. (1994). State, Steel and Strength: Structural Competitiveness and Development in South Korea. *Journal of Development Studies*, 31(1), 44–81.

D'Costa, A. P. (1999) *The Global Restructuring of the Steel Industry: Innovations, Institutions and Industrial Change*. London: Routledge.

D'Costa, A. P. (2009). Economic nationalism in motion: Steel, auto, and software industries in India. *Review of International Political Economy*, 16(4), 620–648.

Dent, C. M. (2000). What Difference a Crisis? Continuity and Change in South Korea's Foreign Economic Policy. *Journal of the Asia Pacific Economy*, 5(3), 275–302.

Dent, C. M. (2003). Transnational capital, the state and foreign economic policy: Singapore, South Korea and Taiwan. *Review of International Political Economy*, 10(2), 246–277.

Diamantopoulos, A., Arslanagic-Kalajdzic, M., and Moschik, N. (2018). Are consumers' minds or hearts guiding country of origin effects? Conditioning roles of need for cognition and need for affect. *Journal of Business Research*. Retrieved from https://doi.org/10.1016/j.jbusres.2018.10.020

Dinnie, K. (2016). *Nation Branding: Concepts, Issues, Practice, 2nd edition*. New York: Routledge.

Dinnie, K., Melewar, T., Seidenfuss, K.-U., and Musa, G. (2010). Nation branding and integrated marketing communications: an ASEAN perspective. *International Marketing Review*, 27(4), 388–403.

Dittmer, L. (2002) Globalization and the twilight of the Asian exceptionalism. In C. Kinnvall and K. Jonsson (Eds), *Globalization and Democratization in Asia: The Construction of Identity*: 21–36. London: Routledge.

Dobbs, R., and Vilinger, R. (2010). Beyond Manufacturing. In M. Company (ed.), *Korea 2020: Global Perspectives for the Next Decade*: 38–51. Korea: McKinsey & Company.

EAAU (1999). *Korea Rebuilds: From Crisis to Opportunity*. Canberra: Department of Foreign Affairs and Trade.

Eckert, C. J., Lee, K.-B., Ick Lew, Y., Robinson, M., and Wagner, E. W. (1990). *Korea, Old and New: A History.* Cambridge, MA: Harvard University Press.

Economist Intelligence Unit (2002). *Magnet or Morass? South Korea's Prospects for Foreign Investment.* Hong Kong: EIU.

El Banna, A., Papadopoulos, N., Murphy, S. A., Rod, M., and Rojas-Méndez, J. I. (2018). Ethnic identity, consumer ethnocentrism, and purchase intentions among bi-cultural ethnic consumers: 'Divided loyalties' or 'dual allegiance'? *Journal of Business Research*, 82, 310–319.

Elliot, S., and Papadopoulos, N. (2016). Of products and tourism destinations: An integrative, cross-national study of place image. *Journal of Business Research*, 69(3), 1157–1165.

Faiola, A., (2004). Court Rejects S. Korean President's Impeachment. *The Washington Post*, May 14, A12.

Fairclough, G. (2005). Free-market Push Divides Korea. *The Wall Street Journal*, November 24, 8.

Fan, Y. (2006). Branding the nation: What is being branded? *Journal of Vacation Marketing*, 12(1), 5–14.

Fitzsimons, G. J., Hutchinson, J. W., Williams, P., Alba, J. W., Chartrand, T. L., Huber, J., … Tavassoli, N. T. (2002). Non-Conscious Influences on Consumer Choice. *Marketing Letters*, 13(3), 269–279.

Frankel, J. (1998). The Asian Model, the Miracle, the Crisis and the Fund. Paper Delivered at the US International Trade Commission, 16 April.

Furlong, H. (2015). Countries Ranked on Sustainable Competitiveness. Retrieved from www.sustainablebrands.com/news_and_views/new_metrics/hannah_furlong/countries_ranked_sustainable_competitiveness_us_uk_score_b.

Gilboa, E. (2008). Searching for a theory of public diplomacy. *The Annals of the American Academy of Political and Social Science*, 616(1), 55–77.

Gilpin, R. (1987). *The Political Economy of International Relations.* Princeton, NJ: Princeton University Press.

Glosserman, B., and Santoro, D. (2012). "The Lynchpin" Grapples with Frustration and Distrust/The Fourth US-ROK Strategic Dialogue, *Issues and Insights*, 12(6), 1–20, February 7.

GMCI (2016). Global Manufacturing Competitiveness Index. Retrieved from www2.deloitte.com/content/dam/Deloitte/us/Documents/manufacturing/us-gmci-skorea.pdf.

Gong, B. H. (1999). The Chaebol – myth and reality. *Business Korea*, 16(10), 34–38.

Govers, R., Go, F. M., and Kumar, K. (2007). Promoting Tourism Destination Image. *Journal of Travel Research*, 46(1), 15–23.

Graham, E. (2005). South Korea must end its corporate xenophobia. *Financial Times*, 4 August 2005.

GSCI (2017). The Global Sustainable Competitive Index, 6th edition. Retrieved from http://solability.com/the-global-sustainable-competitiveness-index/the-index.

Guide, I. W. D. (2017). iF World Ranking. Retrieved from https://ifworlddesignguide.com/if-ranking

Gupta, S., Foroudi, M. M., Väätänen, J., Gupta, S., and Tiu Wright, L. (2018). Nations as brands: Cinema's place in the branding role. *Journal of Business Research*. Retrieved from www.sciencedirect.com/science/article/pii/S0148296318300924

Ha, Y-C., and Lee W. H. (2007). The Politics of Economic Reform in South Korea: Crony Capitalism after Ten Years. *Asian Survey*, 47(6), 894–914.

Haggard, S. (2000). *The Political Economy of the Asian Financial Crisis.* Washington, DC: Institute for International Economics.

Haggard, S., and Moon, C-I. (1983). The South Korean State in the International Economy: Liberal, Dependent, or Mercantile? In John J. Ruggie (Ed.), *The Antinomies of Interdependence*: 131–190. New York: Columbia University Press.

Haggard, S., and Moon, C-I. (1990). Institutions and economic policy: theory and a Korean case study. *World Politics*, 42(2), 210–235.

Haggard, S., Pinkston, D., and Seo, J. (1999). Reforming Korea Inc.: the politics of structural adjustment under Kim Dae Jung. *Asian Perspective*, 23(3), 201–235.

Hair, Joseph F. Jr., Black, William C., Babin, Barry J., and Anderson, Rolph E. (2010). *Multivariate Data Analysis: A Global Perspective*. New Jersey: Pearson Education.

Hall, D. (2004). Japanese spirit, Western economics: the continuing salience of economic nationalism in Japan. *New Political Economy*, 9(1), 79–99.

Han, C. M. (1989). Country Image: Halo or Summary Construct? *Journal of Marketing Research*, 26(2), 222–229.

Han, H. J., and Lee, J. S. (2008). A study on the KBS TV drama Winter Sonata and its impact on Korea's Hallyu tourism development. *Journal of Travel & Tourism Marketing*, 24(2–3), 115–126.

Hanewinkel, R., and Sargent, J. D. (2007). Exposure to Smoking in Popular Contemporary Movies and Youth Smoking in Germany. *American Journal of Preventive Medicine*, 32(6), 466–473.

Hankuk Kyunngje Sinmun (2018) Union is becoming the biggest risk of the national economy. Retrieved from http://news.hankyung.com/article/2018111321741

Harlan, C. (2012). Republic of Samsung. *The Washington Post*, December 9. Retrieved from www.washingtonpost.com/world/in-s-korea-the-republic-of-samsung/2012/12/09/71215420-3de1-11e2-bca3-aadc9b7e29c5_story.html?utm_term=.8936ecebc1f6

Harris, N. (1987) *The End of the Third World: Newly Industrializing Countries and the Decline of an Ideology*. London: I.B. Tauris.

Hart-Landsberg, M., and Burkett, P. (2001). Economic Crisis and Restructuring in South Korea: Beyond the Free Market-Statist Debate. *Critical Asian Studies*, 33(3), 403–430.

Hart-Landsberg, M., Jeong, S., and Westra, R. (2007) *Marxist Perspectives on South Korea in the Global Economy*. Aldershot: Ashgate.

Harvie, C., and Lee, H. H. (2003). Export-led industrialisation and growth: Korea's economic miracle, 1962–1989. *Australian Economic History Review*, 43(3), 256–286.

Heilperin, M. A. (1960). *Studies in Economic Nationalism*. Geneva: Ludwig von Mises Institute.

Helleiner, E. (2002). Economic nationalism as a challenge to economic liberalism? Lessons from the 19th century. *International Studies Quarterly*, 46(3), 307–329.

Herald, K. (2012). Is consumer nationalism relevant today? Retrieved from www.koreaherald.com/view.php?ud=20121029000639

Hofstede, G. (1980). *Culture's Consequences*. Beverly Hills, CA: Sage.

Hofstede, G., and MichaelB. (1984). Hofstede's Cultural Dimensions: An Independent Validation Using Rokeach's Values Survey. *Journal of Cross-Cultural Psychology*, 15(4), 417–433.

Hogarth, H. K. K. (2013). The Korean wave: An Asian reaction to western-dominated globalization. *Perspectives on Global Development and Technology*, 12(1–2), 135–151.

Hong, K. (ed.) (2014). *Nation Branding of Korea*. New York: Palgrave Macmillan.

Hyun, K. J. (2001). Sociocultural change and traditional values: Confucian values among Koreans and Korean Americans. *International Journal of Intercultural Relations*, 25(2), 203–229.

Ih-Prost, O., and Bondaz, A. (2014). South Korea trying to improve its nation brand. Retrieved from www.centreasia.eu/sites/default/files/publications_pdf/note_ka1_south_korea_trying_to_improve_its_nation_brand.pdf

International, E. (2013). South Korea: Largest Market for Men's Skin Care Globally. Retrieved from https://blog.euromonitor.com/2013/06/south-korea-largest-market-for-mens-skin-care-globally.html

Jang, H., and Kim, J. (2002). Nascent stages of corporate governance in an emerging market: Regulatory change, shareholder activism and Samsung Electronics. *Corporate Governance: An International Review*, 10(2), 94–105.

Jang, K. (2018). Between Soft Power and Propaganda: The Korean Military Drama Descendants of the Sun. *Journal of War & Culture Studies*, 1–13.

Jeong, H.-G., and Pek, J.-H. (2016). Special Economic Zones: What Can Developing Countries Learn from the Korean Experience? Retrieved from www.ksp.go.kr/comm on/attdown.jsp?fidx=692&pag=0000700003&pid=209

Johansson, J. K., Ronkainen, I. A., and Czinkota, M. R. (1994). Negative country-of-origin effects: the case of the new Russia. *Journal of International Business Studies*, 25(1), 157–176.

John, J. V. (2017). Korea Peninsula Peace Initiative: Prospects and Challenges of President Moon Jae-in's North Korea Policy. Indian Council of World Affairs. Retrieved from http s://icwa.in/pdfs/VP/2014/KoreaPeaceInitiativeVP31082017.pdf

Johnson, H. G. (1965). A Theoretical Model of Economic Nationalism in New and Developing States. *Political Science Quarterly*, 80(2), 169–185.

Jomo, K. S. (2003). *Globalization, Liberalization and Equitable Development*. Geneva: United Nations Research Institute for Social Development.

Jones, D., and Smith, K. (2005). Middle-earth Meets New Zealand: Authenticity and Location in the Making of The Lord of the Rings. *Journal of Management Studies*, 42 (5), 923–945.

Jones, L., and Sakong, I. (1980). *Government, Business, and Entrepreneurship in Economic Development: The Korean Case*. Cambridge, MA: Harvard University Council on East Asian Studies.

Jonsson, G. (2006). *Towards Korean Reconciliation*. London: Routledge.

Judd, K., and Lee, Y. K. (2000). *An Agenda for Economic Reform in Korea: International Perspectives*. California: Hoover Institution Press.

Jung, T., Graeff, R., and Shim, W. (2011). Good for Samsung is good for Korea: Image restoration strategies used by Samsung after a whistle-blowing corruption scandal. *Open Communication Journal*, 5, 23–29.

Kalinowski, T. (2009). The politics of market reforms: Korea's path from Chaebol Republic to market democracy and back. *Contemporary Politics*, 15(3), 287–304.

Kang, D. C. (2002). *Crony Capitalism: Corruption and Development in South Korea and the Philippines*. Cambridge: Cambridge University Press.

Kang, H. (2015). Contemporary cultural diplomacy in South Korea: Explicit and implicit approaches. *International Journal of Cultural Policy*, 21(4), 433–447.

Kelman, H. C. (1961). Processes of Opinion Change. *Public Opinion Quarterly*, 25(1), 57–78.

Kerr, P., and Wiseman, G. (2013). *Diplomacy in a Globalizing World: Theories and Practices*. New York: Oxford University Press.

Khanna, T., Song, J., and Lee, K. (2011). The paradox of Samsung's rise. *Harvard Business Review*, 89(July-August), 142–147.

Kihl, Y. W. (2005). *Transforming Korean Politics: Democracy, Reform, and Culture: Democracy, Reform, and Culture*. London: Routledge.

Kim, A. E., and Lie, J. (2007). South Korea in 2006: nuclear standoff, trade talks, and population trends. *Asian Survey*, 47(1), 52–57.

Kim, E. Y., Knight, D. K., and Pelton, L. E. (2009). Modeling brand equity of a US apparel brand as perceived by Generation Y consumers in the emerging Korean market. *Clothing and Textiles Research Journal*, 27(4), 247–258.

Kim, F. (2018). A Historical Analysis of Nonmarket Strategy: South Korea. *Academy of Management Proceedings*, 16672. Retrieved from https://doi.org/10.5465/AMBPP. 2018.137

Kim, H., Hoskisson, R. E., Tihanyi, L., and Hong, J. (2004). The evolution and restructuring of diversified business groups in emerging markets: The lessons from chaebols in Korea. *Asia Pacific Journal of Management*, 21(1–2), 25–48.

Kim, J., and Rowley, C. (2001). Managerial problems in Korea – Evidence from the Nationalized Industries. *The International Journal of Public Sector Management*, 14(2), 129–148.

Kim, N. (2016). Youth Culture Is Changing Korea's Coffee. Retrieved from www.neon butmore.com/youth-culture-changing-koreas-coffee/

Kim, S., and Nam, C. (2016). Hallyu Revisited: Challenges and Opportunities for the South Korean Tourism. *Asia Pacific Journal of Tourism Research*, 21(5), 524–540.

Kim, S., Long, P., and Robinson, M. (2009). Small screen, big tourism: The role of popular Korean television dramas in South Korean tourism. *Tourism Geographies*, 11(3), 308–333.

Kim, S. S. (2000). Korea and Globalization (Segyehwa), A Framework for Analysis. In S. S. Kim (ed.), *Korea's Globalization*: 1–28. Cambridge and New York: Cambridge University Press.

Kim, S. S. (2007). Nationalism and Globalization in South Korea's Foreign Policy. *New Asia*, 14(3), 5–48.

Kim, W. S., and Lee, Y-I. (2007). *The Korean Economy: The Challenges of FDI-Led Globalization*. Cheltenham: Edward Elgar.

Kim, W. S., and Kang, H. (1988). Development Strategies and Productivity Issues in Korea, ROC (Taiwan), and Hong Kong: A Comparative Study. In S. Ichimura (ed.), *Challenge of Asian Developing Countries*. Tokyo: Asian Productivity Organisation.

Kim, W-T. (2001). Korean politics: Setting and political culture. In S. H. Kil and C-I. Moon (eds), *Understanding Korean Politics*: 9–32. Albany, NY: State University of New York Press.

Kim, Y. (2011). *The Politics of Coalition in Korea: Between Institutions and Culture*. London: Routledge.

Kim, Y. (2014). The 2012 parliamentary and presidential elections in South Korea. *Electoral Studies*, 34, 326–330.

Kinsey, D. F., and Chung, M. (2013). National Image of South Korea: Implications for Public Diplomacy. *Exchange: The Journal of Public Diplomacy*, 4(1), Article 2.

Kleppe, I. A., Iversen, N. M., and Stensaker, I. G. (2002). Country images in marketing strategies: Conceptual issues and an empirical Asian illustration. *Journal of Brand Management*, 10(1), 61–74.

Klingner, B., and Kim, B. (2007). Economic Lethargy: South Korea Needs a Second Wave of Reforms. *Backgrounder*, 2090, 1–13.

Kong, T. Y. (2000) *The Politics of Economic Reform in South Korea: Fragile Miracle*. London and New York: Routledge.

Korea Associates Business Consultancy (2004). *Profitability of Foreign Companies in Korea: Another Reason to Invest*. Seoul: Korea Associates Business Consultancy.

Korea, S. (2016). Complete Enumeration Results of the 2016 Population and Housing Census. Retrieved from http://kostat.go.kr/portal/eng/pressReleases/8/7/index.board

Korean Economy (2018). Union is becoming the biggest risk of the national economy (in Korean). Retrieved from http://news.hankyung.com/article/2018111321741

Korea FTA Portal (2018). Retrieved from www.customs.go.kr/kcshome/main/content/ContentView.do?contentId=CONTENT_ID_000002801&layoutMenuNo=30710

Krueger, A. (1982). Newly Industrializing Economies. *Economic Impact*, 40(4), 26–32.

Krueger, A. (1990). Government Failures in Development. *Journal of Economic Perspectives*, 4(3), 9–23.

Krugman, P. (1998). Saving Asia: It's Time to Get Radical. *Fortune*, 7 September, 75–80.

KTO (2017). Statistics of Arrivals and Departures. Retrieved from https://kto.visitkorea.or.kr/eng/tourismStatics/keyFacts/KoreaMonthlyStatistics/eng/inout/inout.kto.

Kuznets, P. (1985). Government and Economic Strategy in Contemporary South Korea. *Pacific Affairs*, 58(1), 44–67.

Kwon, O. Y. (2006). Recent Changes in Korea's Business Environment: Views of Foreign Business People in Korea. *Asia Pacific Business Review*, 12(1), 77–94.

Kwon, O. Y. (2010). Impacts of the Korean political system on its economic development: With a focus on the Lee Myung-bak government. *Korea Observer*, 41(2), 189–220.

Lau, H. T., and Lee, R. (2018). Ethnic Media Advertising Effectiveness, Influences and Implications. *Australasian Marketing Journal*, 26(3), 216–220.

Leclerc, F., Schmitt, B. H., and Dubé, L. (1994). Foreign Branding and Its Effects on Product Perceptions and Attitudes. *Journal of Marketing Research*, 31(2), 263–270.

Lee, B., Ham, S., and Kim, D. (2015). The effects of likability of Korean celebrities, dramas, and music on preferences for Korean restaurants: A mediating effect of a country image of Korea. *International Journal of Hospitality Management*, 46, 200–212.

Lee, H.-K. (Ed.) (2013). *Cultural Policy and the Korean Wave*. London: Routledge.

Lee, H. Y. (2004). South Korea in 2003: a question of leadership? *Asian Survey*, 44(1), 130–138.

Lee, K.-T., Lee, Y.-I., and Lee, R. (2014). Economic Nationalism and Cosmopolitanism: A Study of Interpersonal Antecedents and Differential Outcomes. *European Journal of Marketing*, 48(5/6), 1133–1158.

Lee, R., and Lockshin, L. (2012). Reverse Country-of-Origin Effects of Product Perceptions on Destination Image. *Journal of Travel Research*, 51(4), 502–511.

Lee, R., Klobas, J., Tezinde, T., and Murphy, J. (2010). The Underlying Social Identities of a Nation's Brand. *International Marketing Review*, 27(4), 450–465.

Lee, R., Lockshin, L., and Greenacre, L. (2016). A Memory Theory Perspective of Country-Image Formation. *Journal of International Marketing*, 24(2), 62–79.

Levi-Faur, D. (1997). Economic nationalism: from Friedrich List to Robert Reich. *Review of International Studies*, 23(3), 359–370.

LeVine, R. A., and Campbell, D. T. (1972). *Ethnocentrism: Theories of Conflict, Ethnic Attitudes, and Group Behavior*. New York: John Wiley & Sons.

Lie, J. (1998). *Han Unbound: The Political Economy of South Korea*. Stanford, CA: Stanford University Press.

Little, I. (1990). *Economic Development Theory, Policy and International Policy*. New York: Praeger.

Liu, S. S., and Johnson, K. F. (2005). The Automatic Country-of-Origin Effects on Brand Judgments. *Journal of Advertising*, 34(1), 87–97.

Lopez-Aymes, J. F. (2010). Automobile, information and communication technology and space industries as icons of South Korean Economic Nationalism. *Pacific Focus*, 25(2), 289–312.

Ma, Y. S., Song, J.-H., and Moore, D. (2012). Korea's public diplomacy: A new initiative for the future. *The Asian Institute for Policy Studies*, 21(39), 1–25.

MCS (1996). Korea Culture Cultural Identity Selection and Utilization Strategy (in Korean). Retrieved from http://hyongc.net/site/munhwa.htm

Merrilees, B., Miller, D., Ge, G. L., and Tam, C. C. C. (2018). Asian city brand meaning: a Hong Kong perspective. *Journal of Brand Management*, 25(1), 14–26.

Merton, R. (1957). *Social Theory and Social Structure*. New York: The Free Press.

Mikhailitchenko, A., Javalgi, R. G., Mikhailitchenko, G., and Laroche, M. (2009). Cross-cultural advertising communication: Visual imagery, brand familiarity, and brand recall. *Journal of Business Research*, 62(10), 931–938.

Min, B. S. (2006). Trade and Foreign Direct Investment Patterns in the Republic of Korea in the Aftermath of the 1997 Asian Financial Crisis. *Asia-Pacific Trade and Investment Review*, 2(1), 3–24.

Ministry of Commerce, Industry and Energy (MOCIE) (2007). Press Release (in Korean), 4 January.

MOFAT (2010). *Cultural Diplomacy Manual* (in Korean). Retrieved from www.mofa.go.kr

Moon, C-I. (1988). The Demise of a Developmentalist State?: Neoconservative Reforms and Political Consequences in South Korea. *Journal of Developing Societies*, 4, 67–84.

Moon, C-I. (2001). The Kim Dae Jung Government's Peace Policy Toward North Korea. *Asian Perspective*, 25(2), 177–198.

Moon, C-I. (2009). South Korea in 2008: from crisis to crisis. *Asian Survey*, 49(1), 120–128.

Moon, H., Lee, H., and Yoo, G. (1999) *Economic Crisis and its Social Consequences*. Seoul: Korea Development Institute.

Moschis, G. P., and Churchill, Jr., G. A. (1978). Consumer Socialization: A Theoretical and Empirical Analysis. *Journal of Marketing Research*, 15(4), 599–609.

Mossberg, L., and Kleppe, I. A. (2005). Country and destination image – different or similar image concepts? *Service Industries Journal*, 25(4), 493–503.

MSIP (2016). Creative Economy, The Promise of Renovating Korea. Retrieved from http://policy.creativekorea.or.kr/eng/

NBI (2017). Anholt-GfK Nation Brands Index. Retrieved from www.gfk.com/fileadmin/user_upload/2017-11-16_Anholt-GfK_NBI_2017_press_release_global_vfinal.pdf

Nelson, L. C. (2000). *Measured Excess: Status, Gender, and Consumer Nationalism in South Korea*. New York: Columbia University Press.

Nelson, M. R., and McLeod, L. E. (2005). Adolescent brand consciousness and product placements: awareness, liking and perceived effects on self and others. *International Journal of Consumer Studies*, 29(6), 515–528.

Nisbett, R. E., and Wilson, T. D. (1977). The Halo Effect: Evidence for Unconscious Alteration of Judgments. *Journal of Personality and Social Psychology*, 35(4), 250–256.

Njau, B. (2013). Western influence drives South Korean consumer goods industry. Retrieved from www.fdiintelligence.com/Special-Reports/Western-influence-drives-South-Korean-consumer-goods-industry?ct=true

Noland, M. (2005a). Foreign Investors are a Progressive Force. *Korea Times*, 22 September.

Noland, M. (2005b). South Korea's Experience with International Capital Flows. *Working Paper Series, No. 5–4*, Washington DC: Institute for International Economics.

Oberdorfer, D., and Carlin, R. (2013). *The Two Koreas: A Contemporary History*. New York: Basic Books.

O'Connor, N., and Bolan, P. (2008). Creating a sustainable brand for Northern Ireland through film-induced tourism. *Tourism Culture & Communication*, 8(3), 147–158.

OECD (2017). Korea – Economic Forecast Summary. Retrieved from www.oecd.org/korea/korea-economic-forecast-summary.htm

OECD (2018). Development Assistance Committee. Retrieved from www.oecd.org/development/developmentassistancecommitteedac.htm

Onis, Z. (1991). The logic of the developmental state. *Comparative Politics*, 24(1), 109–126.

O'Shaughnessy, J., and O'Shaughnessy, N. J. (2000). Treating the Nation as a Brand: Some Neglected Issues. *Journal of Macromarketing*, 20(1), 56–64.

Padden, B. (2018). Inter-Korean Cooperation Continues As Nuclear Talks Stall. Retrieved from www.voanews.com/a/korea-talks-continue-in-midst-of-denuclearization/4498893.html

Park, C. W., and Lessig, V. P. (1977). Students and Housewives: Differences in Susceptibility to Reference Group Influence. *Journal of Consumer Research*, 5(4), 102–110.

Park, D., and Shin, K. (2012). Performance of the service sector in the Republic of Korea: An empirical investigation. Retrieved from www.adb.org/publications/performance-service-sector-republic-korea

Park, G.-S., Jang, Y. S., and Lee, H. Y. (2007). The interplay between globalness and localness: Korea's globalization revisited. *International Journal of Comparative Sociology*, 48(4), 337–353.

Park, H.-J., Rabolt, N. J., and Sook Jeon, K. (2008). Purchasing global luxury brands among young Korean consumers. *Journal of Fashion Marketing and Management: An International Journal*, 12(2), 244–259.

Park, N. (2017). Moon's Secret Weapon Is Sunshine. Retrieved from https://foreignpolicy.com/2017/05/19/moons-secret-weapon-is-sunshine-south-korea-kim-jong-un/

Park, S.-S. (2018, 28 February). ZARA Korea chief attacked for ridiculing anti-Park protesters. *The Korea Times*. Retrieved from www.koreatimes.co.kr/www/news/biz/2016/11/123_218703.html

Park, T. W. (1999). South Korea in 1998: Swallowing the bitter pills of restructuring. *Asian Survey*, 39(1), 133–139.

PCNB (2009). Presidential Council on Nation Branding. Retrieved from http://17koreabrand.pa.go.kr/gokr/en/cms/selectKbrdCmsPageTbl.do?cd=0124&m1=2&m2=1

Pew Research Centre. (2016). Smartphone Ownership and Internet Usage Continues to Climb in Emerging Economies. Retrieved from www.pewglobal.org/2016/02/22/smartphone-ownership-and-internet-usage-continues-to-climb-in-emerging-economies/

Pharr, J. M. (2005). Synthesizing Country-of-Origin Research from the Last Decade: Is the Concept Still Salient in an Era of Global Brands? *Journal of Marketing Theory and Practice*, 13(4), 34–45.

Pollack, A. (1997). Frugal Koreans rush to rescue their rapidly sinking economy. *New York Times*, December 18, A1. D9.

Porteux, J. N., and Choi, K. J. (2018). Hallyu as Sports Diplomacy and Prestige Building. *Culture and Empathy*, 1(1–4), 70–87.

Poushter, J. (2016). Smartphone Ownership and Internet Usage Continues to Climb in Emerging Economies. Retrieved from www.pewglobal.org/2016/02/22/smartphone-ownership-and-internet-usage-continues-to-climb-in-emerging-economies/

Radelet, S., and Sachs, J. (1998). *The East Asian Financial Crisis: Diagnosis, Remedies, Prospects*. Washington, DC: Brookings Panel.

Ramirez, E. (2017). Nearly 100% Of Households In South Korea Now Have Internet Access, Thanks To Seniors. Retrieved from www.forbes.com/sites/elaineramirez/

2017/01/31/nearly-100-of-households-in-south-korea-now-have-internet-access-thanks-to-seniors/#4603b9cb5572

Rasmussen, R. K., and Merkelsen, H. (2012). The new PR of states: How nation branding practices affect the security function of public diplomacy. *Public Relations Review*, 38(5), 810–818.

Ravenhill, J. (2003). The New Bilateralism in the Asia Pacific. *Third World Quarterly*, 24 (2), 299–371.

Reuters (2016). Drawn by Korean TV drama, 4,500 Chinese tourists gather for chicken, beer. Retrieved from www.straitstimes.com/asia/east-asia/drawn-by-korean-tv-drama -4500-chinese-tourists-gather-for-chicken-beer

Riedel, J. (1988). Economic Development in East Asia: Doing What Comes Naturally? In H. Hughes (Ed.), *Achieving Industrialization in East Asia*: 1–38. Cambridge: Cambridge University Press.

Riefler, P., Diamantopoulos, A., and Siguaw, J. A. (2012). Cosmopolitan consumers as a target group for segmentation. *Journal of International Business Studies*, 43(3), 285–305.

Roach, S. S., and Lam, S. (2010). The resilient economy. In M. Company (ed.), *Korea 2020: Global Perspectives for the Next Decade*: 23–26. London: McKinsey & Company.

Rodier, L. (2014). Assessing the Role of the IMF in South Korea during the Asian Financial Crisis. *Journal of Economics and Development Studies*, 2(2), 107–113.

Ryoo, W. (2009). Globalization, or the logic of cultural hybridization: The case of the Korean wave. *Asian Journal of Communication*, 19(2), 137–151.

Sanidas, E. (2017). Institutional, Political, Economic, and Social Development of South Korea. *The Journal of Social, Political, and Economic Studies*, 42(1), 30–57.

Schröter, T. Y. M., and Schwekendiek, D. (2015). Understanding South Korea's Poor Nation Brand Image: A Content Analysis of Two Leading German Print News Media, 1948–2013. *International Journal of Asia-Pacific Studies*, 11(1), 115–135.

Schütte, H., and Ciarlante, D. (1998). *Consumer Behaviour in Asia*. London: MacMillan Press.

Schwak, J. (2016). Branding South Korea in a Competitive World Order: Discourses and Dispositives in Neoliberal Governmentality. *Asian Studies Review*, 40(3), 427–444.

SCMP (2018). KT wins race in launching world's first 5G service at PyeongChang 2018 Olympics. Retrieved from www.scmp.com/country-reports/business/topics/south-korea-business-report/article/2116061/kt-wins-race-launching

Shimp, T. A., and Sharma, S. (1987). Consumer Ethnocentrism: Construction and Validation of the CETSCALE. *Journal of Marketing Research*, 24(3), 280–289.

Shin, J. (2005). Globalization and Challenges to the Developmental State: A Comparison between South Korea and Singapore. *Global Economic Review*, 34(4), 379–395.

Shin, J.-S. (2005). Substituting and complementing models of economic development in East Asia. *Global Economic Review*, 34(1), 99–118.

Spielmann, N. (2016). Is it all or nothing? Testing schema congruity and typicality for products with country origin. *Journal of Business Research*, 69(3), 1130–1137.

Srinivisan, N., and Jain, S. C. (2003). Country of Origin Effect: Synthesis and Future Direction. In S. C. Jain (Ed.), *Handbook of Research in International Marketing*: 458–476. Cheltenham: Edward Elgar.

Statcounter (2018). Mobile vendor market share Republic of Korea. Retrieved from http://gs.statcounter.com/vendor-market-share/mobile/south-korea

Statistica (2017). Employment by Economic Sector in South Korea. Retrieved from www.statista.com/statistics/604702/employment-by-economic-sector-in-south-korea/

Statistica (2018). International statistics and market data. Retrieved from www.statista.com/markets/422/international/

Steenkamp, J.-B. E. M., and de Jong, M. G. (2010). A Global Investigation into the Constellation of Consumer Attitudes Toward Global and Local Products. *Journal of Marketing*, 74(6), 18–40.

Suh, J. J. (2015). Korea's Democracy After the Cheonan Incident: The Military, the State, and Civil Society Under the Division System. *Asian Perspective*, 39(2), 171–193.

Suisse, C. (2015). Cheil Industries. Retrieved from https://research-doc.credit-suisse.com/docView?language=ENG&source=ulg&format=PDF&document_id=1042703421&serialid=sBh83Dy7tHZqH%2Bb9l4hrjcf1V%2FA%2F0c%2BrJAXgLr7UT%2F4%3D

Thanh, H. P., and Ji, Y. J. (2013). The development of Korea's service industry from a global historical perspective. *International Area Studies Review*, 16(2), 184–205.

The Business Times (2018). Doing business in South Korea getting harder: EU firms. *The Business Times*, 30 January. Retrieved from www.businesstimes.com.sg/government-economy/doing-business-in-south-korea-getting-harder-eu-firms

The Dong-a Ilbo (2007). Survey on 151 foreign invested R&D centres in Korea. Retrieved from http://news.donga.com/3/all/20070529/8447504/1

The World Bank (2015a). GDP per capita (US$) of Korea. Retrieved from https://data.worldbank.org/indicator/NY.GDP.PCAP.CD?locations=KR

The World Bank (2015b). Research and development expenditure (% of GDP). Retrieved from https://data.worldbank.org/indicator/GB.XPD.RSDV.GD.ZS

The World Bank (2016a). Gross National Income (GNI) per capita, PPP. Retrieved from https://data.worldbank.org/indicator/ny.gnp.pcap.pp.cd

The World Bank (2016b). Service, etc., value added (% of GDP). Retrieved from https://data.worldbank.org/indicator/NV.SRV.TETC.ZS?locations=KR

The World Bank (2017). World Development Indicators. Retrieved from http://databank.worldbank.org/data/source/world-development-indicators.

Thompson, C. J., and Tambyah, S. K. (1999). Trying to be cosmopolitan. *Journal of Consumer Research*, 26(3), 214–241.

Tsai, W. S., Yoo, J. J., and Lee, W.-N. (2013). For Love of Country? Consumer Ethnocentrism in China, South Korea, and the United States. *Journal of Global Marketing*, 26(2), 98–114.

UNCTAD (2006). *World Investment Report*. New York: United Nations.

Unit, T. E. I. (2017). Under pressure, South Korean banks are going global. Retrieved from www.eiu.com/industry/article/985812482/under-pressure-south-korean-banks-are-going-global/2017-08-21

van Nooden, R. (2016). South Korea stretches lead in research investment. Retrieved from www.nature.com/news/south-korea-stretches-lead-in-research-investment-1.19333

Verlegh, P. W. J., and Steenkamp, J.-B. E. M. (1999). A review and meta-analysis of country-of-origin research. *Journal of Economic Psychology*, 20(5), 521–546.

Visit Britain (2018). How the World Views Britain – 2018. Retrieved from www.visitbritain.org/britain%E2%80%99s-image-overseas

Volcic, Z. (2008). Former Yugoslavia On the World Wide Web: Commercialization and Branding of Nation-States. *International Communication Gazette*, 70(5), 395–413.

Wade, R. (1988a). State intervention in 'outward-looking' development: Neoclassical theory and Taiwanese practice. In G. White (Ed.), *Developmental States in East Asia*: 30–67. London: MacMillan Press.

Wade, R. (1988b). The Role of Government in Overcoming Market Failure: Taiwan, Republic of Korea and Japan. In H. Hughes (ed.), *Achieving Industrialization in East Asia*: 129–163. Cambridge: Cambridge University Press.

Wade, R. (1990). *Governing the Market: Economic Theory and the Role of Government in East Asian Industrialization*. Princeton, NJ: Princeton University Press.

Wade, R. (1992). Review Article: East Asia's Economic Success–Conflicting Perspectives, Partial Insights, Shaky Evidence. *World Politics*, 44(2), 270–320.

Wästberg, O. (2009). The Symbiosis of Sweden & IKEA. *Public Diplomacy Magazine*, Summer.

Watson, J. J., and Wright, K. (2000). Consumer ethnocentrism and attitudes toward domestic and foreign products. *European Journal of Marketing*, 34(9/10), 1149–1166.

Weiss, L., and Hobson, J. (1998). State Power and Economic Strength: Revisited: What's So Special About the Asian Crisis? Paper presented at the Conference on From Miracle to Meltdown: The End of Asian Capitalism. Asia Research Centre, Murdoch University, Perth, Australia.

Westphal, L. (1978). The Republic of Korea's Experience with Export-led Industrial Development. *World Development*, 6(3), 347–382.

Westphal, L. (1990). Industrial Policy in an Export-propelled Economy: Lessons from South Korea's Experience. *Journal of Economic Perspectives*, 4(3), 41–59.

White, G., and Wade, R. (1988). Developmental states and markets in East Asia: an introduction. In G. White (ed.), *Developmental States in East Asia*: 1–29. London: MacMillan Press.

Wi, T.-W., and Lee, S.-A. (2014). President Park stresses regulation reform, innovation. Retrieved from www.korea.net/NewsFocus/policies/view?articleId=122959

Wilson, E. (2018). Korea's banks want to shine overseas. Retrieved from www.euromoney.com/article/b16bb5njjzksp4/koreas-banks-want-to-shine-overseas

Woo, J. (2017). Political conflicts and democracy after democratization. In Y. Ku, I. Lee and J. Woo, *Politics in North and South Korea*: 49–70. London: Routledge.

Woo, J. E. (1991). *Race to the Swift: State and Finance in Korean Industrialization*. New York: Columbia University Press.

Woo-Cumings, M. (2003). Diverse paths towards the right institutions: law, the state, and economic reform in East Asia. In L. Weiss (ed.), *States in the Global Economy: Bringing Domestic Institutions Back In*: 200–224. Cambridge: Cambridge University Press.

World Trade Organisation (2017). Regional Trade Agreements: Facts and Figures. Retrieved from www.wto.org/english/tratop_e/region_e/regfac_e.htm

Ye, M. (2017). South Korea's Free Trade Strategy and East Asian Regionalism: A Multistage Approach. *Asian Perspective*, 41(1), 147–174.

Yi, J. D. (2002). Globalization and recent changes to daily life in the Republic of Korea. In J. B. Lewis and A. Sesay (Eds), *Korea and Globalization: Politics, Economics and Culture*: 10–35. London: Routledge Curzon.

Yim, H. (2002). Cultural identity and cultural policy in South Korea. *International Journal of Cultural Policy*, 8(1), 37–48.

Yoon, Y-K. (1995). Globalization: toward a new nationalism in Korea. *Korea Focus*, 3(1), 13–28.

Zajonc, R. B. (1968). Attitudinal effects of mere exposure. *Journal of Personality and Social Psychology*, 9(2/Part 2), 1–27.

Zeugner-Roth, K. P., Žabkar, V., and Diamantopoulos, A. (2015). Consumer Ethnocentrism, National Identity, and Consumer Cosmopolitanism as Drivers of Consumer Behavior: A Social Identity Theory Perspective. *Journal of International Marketing*, 23 (2), 25–54.

Index

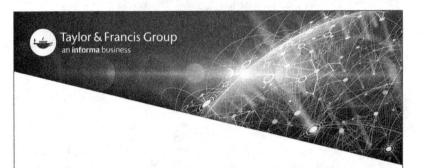

Printed in the United States
by Baker & Taylor Publisher Services